Our Turn
Our Time

WOMEN TRULY COMING OF AGE

edited by cynthia black

BEYOND
WORDS
Publishing
I N C

Beyond Words Publishing, Inc.
20827 N.W. Cornell Road, Suite 500
Hillsboro, Oregon 97124-9808
503-531-8700
1-800-284-9673

Design: Susan Shankin
Composition: William H. Brunson Typography Services
Editors: Cynthia Black and Rosemary Wray
Managing editor: Kathy Matthews

Printed in the United States of America
Distributed to the book trade by Publishers Group West

Library of Congress Cataloging-in-Publication Data
    Our turn, our time : women truly coming of age / edited by Cynthia Black.
       p. cm.
    ISBN 1-58270-029-X (trade paper)
    1 Middle aged women—United States.   2. Aged Women—United States.
3. Aging—United States.   4. Middle ages women—United States—Biography.
5. Aged women—United States—Biography.   I. Black, Cynthia, 1952–
HQ1059.5.U5 O87   2000
305.244—dc21
                                                                    00-028920

The corporate mission of Beyond Words Publishing, Inc.:
  Inspire to Integrity

Contents

Foreword

This book is a gift of permission and promise. Whatever freedom you seek to celebrate, whatever story you wish to speak honestly about women and aging, you will find support here. The voices of many (extra)ordinary women ring strong in these essays, from those who are at the threshold of menopause, to those who remain committed to their quality of life and spirit as the decades tick by.

Even before I began thinking about my own age, I became sensitized through my family's experience to the need to celebrate women's aging. When she was in her early seventies, my mother, Connie, brown-haired, healthy, and vibrant, bemoaned the fact that her grown children were not taking her aging seriously. She had trouble herself taking her own aging seriously, as her mother was still alive (and would live to be 106 years old) and her mother's mother had lived to be 102 years old. Women in my family assume longevity. Rather than thinking at fifty that we are "old," we think we are almost halfway there. So I was surprised to hear my mother longing for this acknowledgment.

That following Christmas, when she and three of her four children and our families were gathered at my brother's house in Minneapolis, we designed a "croning" ritual similar to celebrations recounted throughout this book. In the decade since, I have watched my mother assume a leadership role among her peers that she credits over and over again to that simple ceremony. "I am a crone," I hear her say in various gatherings. "I have something to say ... I have the authority of years ... I have perspective...."

Since my work brings me into close connection with hundreds of women each year, I have learned to listen to all of us speak the wisdom of our ages—from girls to elders. If I could sum up what I learn from women over and over again, it would be the reminder—

It's always the right time to claim our power.
It's always the right time to tell our story.
It's always the right time to find people who can really hear us.

These are the lessons that ring in each of the essays in this book. And the experience that most often supports women as we claim power, tell story, and hear each other occurs when we come into a circle. The word "circle" and the description of this ceremonial space permeate this book.

Circle seems an innately women's way of gathering. We cluster around kitchen tables, coffee tables, conference tables. We pull chairs together to work with our hands and to talk, to serve on committees, boards, task forces and teams, and to help keep the world functioning in a million tender ways. Whether or not we claim to be "in circle," these acts reconnect us to a tradition that is tens of thousands of years old; a heritage that extends back to the cooking fires and council fires of our ancestors. As we claim our turn and take our time, the circle holds us within a sacred space where we can share stories and experience.

While women's intuitive "circling up" has enriched many of us with exquisite moments of intimacy and shared spirit, the circle can also be an experience that unleashes confusion and mistrust. Some of the stories in this book teach us these harder lessons. The circle is an interpersonal art form and it will mirror back to us both the exquisite beauty and surprise of our relationships, and the difficulties of understanding and knowing how to be with each other. However, the circle has a tensile strength, and I love and honor the circle. I celebrate its source, strength, and adaptability. I believe the circle has always served as, and remains, the core of community. Wherever the circle is used, in all the settings where council may be called, there are simple yet essential structures that help us be in circle in safe and respectful ways. Many of the essays here remind us how to sit in circle.

One of the ways in which you are invited to use this book is to find some women with whom you believe you can mutually claim power, tell story and listen, and call a circle to read this book together.

Then circle by circle, women may practice *being* the changes we want to create in the world. We may bear witness to each other. We may teach each other what we know about aging. We may rise together in communities with a sense that we are not alone. We are many.

Christina Baldwin is the author of Calling the Circle, the First and Future Culture, *published by Bantam in 1998. She trains circle leaders and consults with groups who wish to shift into council. In 1994 she and her partner, Ann Linnea, moved to Washington State and founded PeerSpirit, Inc. In Service to the Circle. She is a practical visionary who believes the circle leads people to spirit-based social action. She can be reached through her website, www.peerspirit.com, or at Box 550, Langley, WA 98260 USA.*

A Note from the Editor

When I was growing up in the 1950s, with my grandmother and great-grandmother as my models of aging women, it was inconceivable to me that I would ever be as old as they seemed to be. As I now approach the age of fifty, I realize that I am the same age as my grandmother was back then, but it feels as if being fifty is very different for me than it was for her.

My friends have noticed this too—our clothes, our body sense, our expectations, and our levels of activity have changed. We have few models from the past. We are creating as we go. And so it is important that we communicate our ideas, support each other, question authority, and laugh together. That's why this book came into being. It is indeed our turn, our time.

Because I have learned so much over the last few years from talking with, observing, listening to, and reading about inspiring, courageous, and creative women, I wanted to be a part of this adventure of creating new models. As a publisher, I put out an invitation for women over fifty to submit their writing for a collective book of women's wisdom. Women from many ways of life sent wonderful pieces of writing. This book shares with you just some of the stories and ideas about talking and connecting; about art, literature, music, and dance; about the wonderful new energy that emerges during and after menopause; about the deepening spirituality that women can share; and about practical ideas for living with the challenges, the joys, and the transitions we all face.

I would like to invite you to participate by reading this book, talking with other women, learning more about the writers represented here, and maybe writing about your own adventures for another collection of *Our Turn, Our Time* stories. Think of this book as a virtual women's circle inviting you to participate at any level you wish — it is also your turn, your time.

CYNTHIA BLACK

EDITOR

Our Turn, Our Time

GAIL BALDEN

Over the last few years, Gail Balden has been reclaiming her creative spirit and has begun to pursue the things that bring her joy, passion, and meaning: her writing, her teaching of writing workshops for women, her work in theater, and her focus on spiritual growth. She likes to push her envelope of comfort with adventurous activities such as Outward Bound trips, backpacking, and bicycling, including riding across the state of Michigan at age fifty-five and every year since. She directs and acts in plays, teaches creative expression at the local community college, and has formed a writing group. She has had her writing published in RAIN, Poetry and Prose Annual, *and many local magazines.*

Your Life in Two Words

Imagine distilling your entire life and purpose to just two words, like *Lassoing Dreams, Reigning Wit, Seeking Wisdom, Tendering Heart, Soaring Inspiration, Discovering Treasures, Unearthing Truth, Making Waves* — words that encompass all of who you are deep down, words that lift you up, words that are rich and playful, full of joy and life. These are the names a group of eight women ages forty-one to seventy-two have chosen for themselves with one another's help. They are part of a group which began as a ten-week class called "Creative Calisthenics."

"Calisthenics" is made up of the Greek word "kalos," which means "beautiful," and "sthenos," which means "strength." *Beautiful strength* is what this group of women have developed over a period of a year and a half, in meetings held first at the local community college and then in their homes. When they come together for one of their last meetings, I am invited to attend.

Always on the lookout for clues as to what we women are all about, I am curious. Oh, I've had my leaps of faith in the last seven years, things I never thought I'd do after the age of fifty—finally getting serious about my writing and getting it published, starting a writing workshop business, taking an Outward Bound trip, making three bicycle trips across Michigan with my sister and daughter. I even picked up a paintbrush and faced the naked canvas, something I had never done before. But what is it with us women, with this yearning for creative expression, this longing for depth and meaning and for living authentic lives?

The women bring their final projects to the gathering, and the room is filled with glorious objects of art—copper sculpture, collages, haiku, mosaics, charcoal drawings, fish prints, woven baskets, and handmade paper. I am in awe. These women are happy, ageless, glowing with creative spirit. Intrigued by their joy and vitality, I ask what has prompted them to join a group called Creative Calisthenics, to step into the darkness of the unknown, poised on the brink of who knew what.

Listen in on parts of the conversations:

Nan, forty-one, architectural designer: "The last year and a half has broadened my world. It gave me a sense of who I am. It opened me up."

Debi, forty-five, chef: "There are so many choices in deciding what to play with as a creative woman. This group transcends age; it makes no difference. We are together in time. Life is getting better as I get older, more creative, and more spiritual. I love seeing that life can be richer and more beautiful as we get older."

Margie, forty-six, business owner: "This group got me writing again and inspired me to go back to college and finish my degree."

Ann, seventy-two, retired elementary-school teacher: "I am a happier person for having done all this. I feel I have blossomed. The last year has opened me up to so many possibilities in all ways. It lightens me up to see everyone's creative work."

Alisa, forty-one, college administrator: "Looking at others' work for inspiration is wonderful. It has helped me develop other ways of being."

Jane, sixty-two, retired schoolteacher: "Retirement sounds like stopping; instead, it's a beginning, a wide-open world."

Norma, sixty-five, retired: "Being with this group of women aroused my creative spirit; I feel a special bond with each woman in the group."

Lorraine, forty-three, graphic designer, yoga instructor, and teacher of this class: "My life has been enriched a millionfold by the women in this group. I was craving this in my life, and now it is spilling over and over. It's all about practice. You're never really done. That 'undoneness' takes us back to the practice again and again."

Believing that she is in the world to help people be more creative, the leader of the group, Lorraine (Lassoing Dreams), says she's really been preparing to teach a Creative Calisthenics class for the last forty years. She sees creativity as a muscle, and "like all muscles, it needs to be strengthened." At some point in her own journey, Lorraine says, she was asked what her story is, and she realized it is "Cowgirl Moves to Pacific Northwest and Starts the Art Ranch." So she moved from California to the Pacific Northwest and started the Art Ranch, an enterprise that cultivates, supports, and produces creative projects of all kinds. She designed the Creative Calisthenics class to provide a structured environment where women could take risks, receive positive support, try new things, play, and strengthen their creative spirits—knowing there was no right or wrong way, and that they could not fail.

Lorraine says, "I feel that I'm a guide, leading people into the wilderness. I'm the person at the front of the group carrying a huge torch, encouraging them to cross chasms, supporting them, and encouraging them to reintegrate creativity into their lives slowly, so that it becomes a manageable and gradual process. One of the things I asked them to do early on was to write poems about where unmet dreams reside. The results of this were juicy and powerful—they took us underneath what was known and revealed deep, unspoken truths. With these, we were poised and ready to begin our journey. And so we did. Week after week, as we took more and more risks, let ourselves dream, listened to our intuition and experienced the joy of doing something just for the pleasure of it, we became really strong."

"How does this overlap and slip into their work lives and the community?" I asked.

"In all kinds of ways," Lorraine responded. "I see these women being more available and open to people and new ideas, more nurturing in their jobs and lives, happier people. I see women using their creativity in new ways. They are painting their rooms red, writing books, going back to college, taking risks, taking their newborn confidence out into the community, their churches, their volunteer work with the elderly and young people. They have created vitality for moving into the juiciest part of their lives—singing until the moment they die, living an authentic life. I tell them it's a lifelong practice."

The women agree that creativity is ageless and doesn't need to ebb as one gets older. Ann (Reigning Wit), the eldest in the group at seventy-two, says, "Creativity is always in us, yet very few women of my generation pursued art. I think it makes you feel younger. You can be over seventy and still have a good time. So you don't have to think that when you get to fifty, it's the end. In all my creative endeavors, I feel I am expressing my soul. And it affects everything in my life. It spreads out all around and is a unifying thing." Ann volunteers at the local district attorney's office in the Victims' Advocacy Program, reads stories to children at the library, volunteers at the elementary school, and is an avid ocean and river kayaker. "All my creative endeavors have given me a wonderful sense of self." Like many women who have a passion for beauty, and who express this in the creation of a home, Ann says, "I love setting a lovely table, whether anyone comes for dinner or not."

Debi (Discovering Treasures) thinks being in a group of women of different ages has given her an appreciation of their diversity and their different perceptions and twists on things. "It has opened me up to learning something from each one of them. Though I am forty-five, I still feel like I'm twenty, and I'm getting more and more comfortable with doing less and less. I like the feeling of being grounded in creative activity at home, knowing I have the support of other creative women whether I am with them or not. It is very comforting and satisfying and reduces my needs. Life is more simple, and I don't need as much to be happy. We have been raised with cultural images that tell us if we are young, thin, and beautiful, we have worth. That we will be discarded as we get older. But life keeps blossoming. New things can open up to us. It's like dropping a pebble in water; the ripples keep going. I think we women are getting over the notion that we have to look a certain way or be a certain way. We are beginning to realize that anything is possible at any age. More and more women are climbing out of their boxes."

Debi says she believes the world does not encourage artists, yet it is creativity that feeds her soul and connects her with people. "I live in connection, on an intimate level, with other women, and can spend time alone and not feel I'm alone. My contentment comes from an inner sense of worth, which feeds and strengthens my sense of self." Pointing to her truck in the driveway, Debi is hardly able to contain her excitement. It is filled with scrap copper tubing just waiting for her to create her next sculpture.

Jane (Tendering Heart) says the class inspired her to write her first song. "When I visualize myself as a child, I see myself at age eight at the piano. I have learned to reclaim that early love, to take more risks and be comfortable with going ahead and experiencing joy. The support of the group, and Lorraine's openness and commitment to bringing support and safety into an encouraging environment, made all the difference." Jane entered the Trash Art show, a local exhibition of art made with recycled materials. Along with three other women from the group, Jane submitted her first artistic rendering of found objects. Jane says the strengthening of her creative spirit carries over into the way she lives her life — caring about her community, volunteering at school, and substituting in the classroom. "There are so many ways to be alive and not just work."

Norma (Seeking Wisdom) believes creativity can encompass anything, not just the arts. "I feel one is an artist even though she doesn't produce 'art.' It's a way of being, of living your life." Norma says she feels that the older women in the group learn from the younger ones and that it's all right to be positive about themselves. "For me, there is a sense of urgency as I age, but also a feeling of freedom. Regardless of our age, we are valuable to ourselves and to others."

Margie (Unearthing Truth) says being a part of this group of women has changed her entire life. Admitting that she likes to explore new things, she changed her work schedule so that she could take Lorraine's class. She loved the class so much that she cut back her work hours even more, so that she would have more time in her life to create. She credits the class with opening her up to writing again. She wants to go back to college and finish the degree that she started oh, so long ago, before she married, before she made pots for years, before she had a child at thirty-nine and forgot how much she loved to write and paint. She says she had not painted a picture since junior high school, but she entered a local art show and was very pleased with her painting. "It was really quite good!" she exclaims. She now finds herself exploring all kinds of artistic expression. "I realized I can make space for creativity in my life. Age is not a factor in this group; the older women are in great shape physically and mentally and exemplify that aging is something to celebrate. I think there is a fear of getting older, of running out of time. This is the best decade of my life. The course of my life has changed. I had this talent once, and I realize it's not gone; I can still do this."

Nan (Soaring Inspiration), the youngest in the group at forty-one, says she went on her feelings of trust when signing up for Creative Calisthenics. "I needed to rejuvenate my creative juices. I had no idea where it would go or that I would explore new territory where fear was not a factor. For me, curiosity is stronger than fear. I feel I'm more creative since being in this group. It has opened up a whole new world for me. I even wrote a book of poetry! Since becoming part of this group, I know myself better; I'm stronger and have a much better sense of self. Lorraine was like a soft blanket over all of us, encouraging us to listen to our dreams and bring them to reality."

One of Nan's dreams was to stay overnight at a bookstore. "You can never spend too much time in a bookstore," Nan says. "So we got permission from the owner, and we spent the night. One woman slept by the self-help books, thinking maybe she'd get some help while she slept. That's the only time when age became a factor because Ann, the eldest, wanted to go to bed early." Nan laughs. "The older women in the group were an inspiration to me and helped me see that anything is possible. Dream the dream, and it's possible. That's what I've learned from this group."

Alisa (Making Waves) says she became involved because the notion of stretching her creative muscle resonated with her. "I know that playfulness is a necessary component in my life. When I feel stuck, if I can find a playful approach to a problem, I find flow. What I learned in this group is that it's not about right or wrong, it's about diving in." Alisa says she feels that all of our experiences overlap into our life and our work to transform who we are. "They become part of our little bag of tricks." She was particularly delighted with the way each of the women in the group approached the creative exercises. "There seemed to be a certain grace and calmness in the approach of the older women. I felt like I had these playmates of all ages. There was such encouragement to try the untried path."

One of the assignments was to give a dinner party for their creative spirits, and to set a table with objects that represented their deepest selves. Alisa says she walked through her house and chose things that appealed to her. "One of the things I chose was a packet of various colors of tissue paper. I had no idea what I was going to do with it. But when I asked each of the women to pick a color that appealed to her, when I put on music and told them we were now wind, and we were going to dance with the tissue paper, they all did it! And the ones who seemed to enjoy it the most were the older women. To be so embraced by a group of such women was a powerful and moving experience."

Alisa says one of the best things to come out of the group was the opportunity to teach one of the sessions. "With Lorraine's encouragement, each of us chose an area in which we felt we could lead the class. For me, it created a full circle, going from student to teacher and back to student. For each of us to have the opportunity to teach was like having a spotlight turned on us at various times; it was a delight and an inspiration. I taught the group how to make copper sculpture, not because I knew that much about it, but because I knew how to solder. I once saw a five-foot copper sprinkler at a wedding; when I said I wanted one just like it, I was told to make it. So I did. I'm a single woman with no children, but when I see these women out there creating artistic expression with copper sculpture, something that I taught them, it's like seeing my children and grandchildren in the world."

By the time I leave the women I am inspired by their creative juices. I am enthralled with the idea of women of mixed ages discovering that age makes no difference; that the mix of youth and age only brings about a greater combination of freshness, vitality, and experience. I like the ritual the women conduct each time they meet, the roundtable check-in, when each is asked what she has done to nurture her creative spirit since they last met. I like the idea of women sharing their talents, telling their stories, developing strong creative spirits in their practices, replacing ego with inspiration, getting in touch with their spirituality, taking risks, and crashing through walls of their own making to explore and try new things in a supportive environment. I like being with women who have discovered the joy of who they are, who know that what matters more than age is whether or not they are strengthening their creative spirits, living authentic lives, and remaining faithful to their practice.

Lassoing Dreams, Reigning Wit, Seeking Wisdom, Tendering Heart, Soaring Inspiration, Discovering Treasures, Unearthing Truth,

Making Waves. What would it be like if we all distilled our lives and purpose to just two words that represented who we really are; if we lived our lives from our joyful hearts; if we valued our intentions, banished the negative, let go of fear, and leapt—knowing the net would appear. What would it be like? I think the world would split wide open.

JO BARNEY

Jo Barney is a graduate of Willamette University in Salem, Oregon, and the women described in her story were all fellow students forty years ago. Jo is a wife, mother, stepmother, schoolteacher, school counselor, and now, finally, writer, which she knew she would become even as she was accepting all of these other roles. She has written one novel, is working on the next, and has published essays and articles over the years. Jo loves her new resume, which says "Jo Barney: Writer."

a Reluctant Crone

It might have been the candlelight or the moment, but each of us in the circle was beautiful, a golden glow blooming at our cheeks, our eyes deep and mysterious.

We had gathered at my beach house on a lark. "Come," I had written, "and let's celebrate our ascent into cronehood." At the time, I wasn't sure what I meant, either about the celebration or the ascent. I just knew I was feeling old—sixty years old—and I wanted to see some friends.

June wrote back, "This doesn't mean whoo-whoo (I could hear her voice, whooing) stuff, does it?" I looked uneasily at the six blue candles I had bought with just a little whoo-whoo in mind. My four other invitees, college buddies turned women friends of forty years, replied that they looked forward to an old-fashioned slumber party. "But 'crones'?" Judy wondered. "Isn't that a bit harsh? That may be you, but it ain't me, friend."

Despite the hint of negativity I was picking up from the responses, I couldn't shake the need for some sort of celebration, some way to mark this place in the curve of our lives. So I looked for help in the bookstore down the street.

There it was. "Crone," holding down a respectable spot next to "Co-dependency," right down the shelf from "Affirmations." I pulled out a book and began to page through it.

"Wise woman . . . a healer, midwife to new experiences." That had a positive note, well worth celebrating, I thought. And then I found ". . . old wise woman who watches over dreams and visions, who whispers secrets to our inner ears." A little whoo-ey, but real-life. I'd had some experience trying to whisper into a daughter-in-law's ear.

I kept reading:

> The Crone, in modern days, represents the woman who is able to pare all that is alienating and confining from the self— the false selfs from the Self . . . like the silkworm, spinning fibers around herself and later emerging as something new.

Yes! The thought of emerging as something new at this point in my life overwhelmed me, as I quickly jotted down what I had read. In my exitement I put the book back on the shelf willy-nilly, not even taking the time to note authors and titles. I could hardly wait to get home to call Judy. She'd like it, too.

After dinner, the six of us gathered around the blue candles in front of the fireplace, wineglasses and reading glasses at hand. We began with a smattering of crone magic to get us in the mood. I offered my findings on a *Charm to Cure the Body of Sundry Ailments*, involving beeswax and a ribbon of silk ("Really?" June asked) and a *Charm for Eternal Youth*, requiring a stand of pine trees, a moonlit night, and pine needles strung on a green thread. ("I can do that!" June exulted, whoo-whooing a little).

Then we moved inward, the candlelight beckoning. One after another, we opened our books and read aloud.

Jill gave us *Ithaca*:

Arriving there is what you are destined for.
But do not hurry the journey at all.
Better if it lasts for years,
so that you are old by the time you reach the island.
(Constantine P. Cavafy)

Pat reminded us of our friendship, with "The Pleasures of an Ordinary Life."

...A long history.
Connections that help render us complete.
Ties that hold and heal us. And the sweet,
Sweet pleasures of an ordinary life.
(Judith Viorst)

And through *Comes the Dawn*, Ann spoke of our growing sense of selfhood:

After a while you learn that even sunshine
Burns if you get too much,
So you plant your own garden and decorate

Your own soul, instead of waiting

For someone to bring you flowers.

(Veronica Shoffstall)

Then Judy recalled a poem her father had written as he reflected on his own old age. "There's a song to be sung," he advised, sounding so much like his forever optimistic daughter that we all smiled.

As the blue candles dripped lovely, free-flowing ponds across the top of the old chest, we came to the end of our ceremony. Each of us held in her palm an object she had combed from the beach that afternoon, in searching for a symbol of herself. An agate, a tiny clamshell, a piece of driftwood, a baby crab, grains of sand, a curling hank of seaweed. In the flickering light, in the listening silence, we each spoke of our treasures and of ourselves: our dreams, our fears, our understandings of our worlds. Whispering secrets for inner ears, I realized. It came to us so naturally, as if we had been preparing for these revelations forever.

We didn't stay up all night, the way we might have in college, although we did wander about in our nightgowns for a while, not wanting the evening to end. When the last crone had found her bed, I turned off the lights and headed for mine. "I liked the part about the old woman spinning, Wisdom herself, spinning and weaving the thread of life," my bed partner June murmured, her voice muffled by her pillow. "That could be me."

"I think it's all of us," I answered, but she was asleep already.

JANIS BARRETT

Janis Barrett was raised on a sheep and cattle ranch in southcentral Montana. Currently, she spends her leisure time trail-riding in Montana's beautiful mountains, learning to paint Montana's scenery, and traveling. She also volunteers for Habitat for Humanity. At present she is working on a children's book in which the main character is based on her daughter. Her grown son, who practices law, has escaped being involved in her literary adventures. Janis lives in Bozeman, with her husband, Steve, her English setters, Kelsey and Shelby, and her horses, Duke and Pal.

Out of the Grandstand and Onto the Field

I'm not thirty years old anymore! This fact became obvious to me one day in the Safeway store as I observed a woman with three little kids in tow. One was in the basket of the grocery cart, gumming animal crackers, and the older two were perusing the aisles and bringing inappropriate choices back to Mom, with whiny questions: "Can we have this, pu-u-l-lease, Mommy, please?" Those kids gave me sharp pangs of memory and a realization that when I went through this, it was sixteen or seventeen years ago.

At fifty-four, memories of raising my family and reflections on life in general seem to occupy a lot of my time. Trying to assign value to what I have been doing for the last thirty-one years as a married woman, and the last fifty-four years as a human being, gives me plenty to think about as I go about my day-to-day life.

You understand, I was on the cusp of the feminist revolution — born too soon to be a career woman, and too late to justify being a stay-at-home mom. Easily the most irritating question about my life comes from the new acquaintance who inquires, "So, Janis, what do you do?" This question angers me, because in my heart of hearts, I am satisfied with what I do in my life. So, lately I have started replying that I am a kept woman. That usually shuts people up. One woman actually asked me how I managed to be kept. She wanted to know, and to position herself to be the same. It was a serious question!

So what *do* I do?

I spent the child-rearing years observing my tasks and duties as if I were watching plays in a baseball game from a seat at Dodger Stadium. It was as if I were in the grandstand watching my life happen. I have looked for the reason I felt so removed from my life. Perhaps I felt that contemporary culture did not reflect my goals and desires. Perhaps I was just so busy meeting everyone else's needs that I didn't have time to think of myself as an individual with her own needs. I was cook, soccer mom, laundress, psychologist—all of those daily things that take time, energy, and commitment. I made costumes for school plays, baked for bake sales, hauled loads of pre-teens to rock concerts and stayed to listen to music that made my ears ring for two days. As I look back, it seems that I performed these tasks in a haze. It was just my job. The trouble was, there was no boss, no office, and no one signing a paycheck.

I thought that a paycheck was the only way to measure myself against the women who ran their own businesses, taught school, or worked as secretaries. Most mornings I read the classified section, hoping to find a job that had my name on it. Literally, my name. It was approach-avoidance at its finest. I couldn't figure out how I would balance a job with all the stuff I did at home. I had a big garden, lots of flowers, and a huge lawn. I also ran the kids to doctors, sports practices, and music lessons. I prided myself on clean floors and good, balanced meals. But the question remained: what do I do?

About the time my daughter was a junior in high school, I knew I would have to reorder my life. My husband and I were finally able to go out for dinner or to a movie spontaneously, without planning for a sitter. We enjoyed our fledgling state of freedom. We became reacquainted with ourselves and our friends. Our weekends were spent skiing, riding horses, entertaining, and occasionally eating and drinking too much. It was terrific to be irresponsible again. I only occasionally asked myself, "What do I do?" I finally felt that I was actually participating in life and not just observing it. The nest was going to be totally empty very soon, and I was going to be ready for fun.

Concurrently, my aging parents were relying on me more and more for decisions, transportation, and company. Having roles reverse and caring for those who cared for you can be unnerving. It has been an important stage of my life and has helped me understand many things about myself. I have learned the value of physical contact. I am learning to slow down. I have learned about simplicity. I know that the old stories are a way for me to connect with my history. It is a fact that I think of Mom and Dad before I plan events in my new days as an empty-nester.

I wonder if Mom ever thought about her newly acquired freedom when I left home and married. We are thirty-three years apart in age, and when Mom was in her mid-fifties she was still working, as she always had.

Mom and Dad always worked. Their days started early in the morning and ended late at night. Mom cooked three meals a day—big meals for hired hands. She ran the domestic side of their operation: She gardened, butchered chickens, preserved fruits and vegetables, and sewed patches on overalls. She learned how to keep the books for the ranch. She painted and cleaned and maintained. Occasionally she helped with farming and ranching chores. There wasn't much time for socializing or self-fulfillment.

Dad ran cattle, sheep, and, occasionally, some pigs. He hayed, irrigated, fixed machinery, mended fences, and attended church.

Together my parents brought me up to the best of their ability. It was strict, religious, and rural. My add-a-bar-a-year Sunday School attendance pin was about four inches long by the time I reached confirmation age. I was a 4-H member in good standing. I learned to cook, sew, raise animals, wire a lamp, and garden. I think it was expected that I would marry the boy next door, and that the two ranches would be combined.

I had other ideas. I wanted to go to college. My father has an eighth-grade education, and Mom finished high school. Her only work experience away from home was in summer 1932 in Seattle. She worked as a maid for a Norwegian family. It was called "being in service." I didn't think that I would ever, under any circumstances, "be in service," or that I would marry the boy next door for the purpose of increasing land holdings.

When I graduated from high school, my parents conceded that it would be OK (just OK) for me to attend college—the land-grant college. I was to learn to be a teacher or a nurse. Those fields were appropriate for women and conducive to working until I met the proper husband. There was only one role model with a higher education in our extended family, an uncle who had gone to a polytechnic school.

I did, however, have a wonderful English teacher in high school who encouraged me to apply to Northwestern University School of Journalism. But I was too scared to make such a giant leap. It was so far away. I was even too scared to go to the University of Montana to major in journalism. Too far away from home—the career choice was too iffy.

So, in 1963, I packed my sweater sets, straight skirts (homemade), and cotton dresses, and left for the land-grant college a hundred miles from home. John F. Kennedy was assassinated that fall, and it seemed that the world had gone crazy, even though we in Bozeman were isolated from a lot of the turmoil. It was during the college years that I began to feel like an observer of my own life. Those years, from late 1963 to spring 1967, were the first time I occupied that seat at Dodger Stadium to spectate at my own life.

The question at that time was, "What am I going to be when I grow up?" After four years, and no changes of major, no questions about what really interested me or what I could do, I graduated with a Bachelor of Science in Home Economics, with a business option. I purposely didn't get teaching credentials, because I was going to do this *my* way. At twenty-two, I finally had enough gumption to get a job in Los Angeles in the retail training program of a large department store. I thumbed my nose at nursing and teaching.

I had my first furnished apartment under the landing pattern at LAX! It had an uncomfortable brown Naugahyde couch, and the building rattled with the sound of the landing planes.

I was so homesick. It felt so strange going to work every day. I had never had a career woman working outside the home for a role model. I didn't like the training program, and felt that the company was just using the trainees for whatever tasks they couldn't find employees for. I made few friends, and hardly had a social life at all. I was back at Dodger Stadium watching the game again!

I had been dating a fellow student the summer after graduation, and his plans were to go to law school in Washington, D.C. Money—the lack of it—landed him in L.A. looking for a job, while his acceptance at George Washington School of Law was put on hold for a year. Steve and I continued our relationship, and that year, at Christmas, he asked me to marry him. I said yes; we called our folks, and set a date in May 1968. I felt that my life was finally going to start. I also felt that my career was finally going to end. I had no remorse.

I didn't check with Mom and Dad to see if they approved of the match. After all, I was marrying a Catholic city slicker who smoked and drank and didn't have calluses on his hands.

Two years after we were married, I encountered my first "liberated woman" at a dinner party. She was a large, strident creature whose mousy husband wore the worst toupee imaginable. She loudly discussed equal pay, women's rights, Gloria, and other icons of the women's movement. It was funny—she personified the stereotypical, emasculating bra burners that many people felt *were* the women's movement. That night, I registered her impact on me as neither negative nor positive. But I do think that she gave me something to think about.

I was a young mother by this time, and I suddenly looked at my beautiful infant son in a new way—he was my incarceration, and the term looked like it was going to be for the next twenty years or so. I was back at Dodger Stadium, observing myself playing the game of new mother/wife. I realized that there must be more to life than diapers, strained carrots, and walks around the block with the stroller.

I thought of taking more college classes to give me some kind of practical background so that I could get a job. But I was rooted to the ground. I couldn't make myself leave my home and my children. I was living my mother's life, and I was totally unfulfilled. I have never asked her if she had feelings like mine. She may have been too busy even to think about such issues.

After my daughter was born, it was becoming quite clear to me that I was bringing up my kids in much the same way that I had been brought up, and that I was conducting my life in much the same way that my parents had conducted theirs. I couldn't reconcile my life as a lawyer's wife with this rural past of mine. Every time I was faced with a social situation, I felt the meadow muffin syndrome rear its head. I wanted to keep those 1950s rural values, and to ignore the fact that there was money to spend—that we lived a privileged existence. I enrolled the kids in 4-H, which they thought was a big waste of time. I encouraged them to be good citizens and to try to include some charitable work in their lives. They didn't much buy into that, either. I enforced a curfew, and grounded or punished them for mis-behavior. It was a lot of work!

I learned a lesson from a good friend, almost too late in the child-rearing business. She said, "You have got to learn to pick your battles." Then I learned something else from my brother-in-law. He said,

"Don't attach all the hopes and aspirations of two people to your child — it's too much for one person to carry."

With the influence of my parents, my friends and family, and a lifestyle far different from what I had ever imagined, I was still waiting for the answer to the question, "What *is* it that *I* do?"

The answer isn't completely clear, even now that my children are grown. They tell me that what I did made a difference. They have both told me how important it was to have someone at home when they came home from school. They both acknowledge that I had a positive impact on their lives. My daughter considers me a strong role model.

I have volunteered my time and energy to many of the usual charities. It is still my message to my kids to reach outside of oneself and make a contribution that means something to someone else.

The time I spend with my aging parents has taken on more meaning. They are happy in their routine in their small town. I appreciate that they are able to care for themselves with a minimum of outside help. Their gerontologist said, "They are poster children for old age." I am very grateful for that.

Owning and training horses has returned me to my rural roots. I find joy in the time I spend riding or just fiddling with my animals. Horses have allowed me to acknowledge my background. They have also forced me to relax and not take my harried life to the corral.

My garden delights me. It renews my faith in life and living to be able to sow seeds and collect a harvest. I like the positive feedback from the friends who receive my vegetable and flower gifts. Gardening also helps me to acknowledge my roots.

I've taught myself to quilt and have made gifts for many people. I have kept only one of my creations for myself, because I find that I like to give away parts of me.

Only occasionally in social situations do I find myself back in the seat at Dodger Stadium, watching my life. Self-doubt evaporates over time and with varied experience.

It isn't possible to recite your various interests and avocations to someone who asks the obnoxious question, "What do you do?" There is no pat answer. I do what it takes to make me happy with myself. I work to develop the part of me with whom I like to spend time alone. I acknowledge the importance of my husband, my parents, my children, and my friends.

If I haven't been able to fully define what it is that I do, I find that I am learning to know who I am—and that is, perhaps, the answer after all. I am glad to be fifty-four and filled with wisdom, and equally glad that the insurance tables tell me there should be at least twenty-five more years left in which to get to know myself better. This is, perhaps, the time of life for moving onto the playing field—the late afternoon sun is warm and bright, and I am finally playing the game of life, and not watching it from the grandstand.

B.J. BATEMAN

B.J. Bateman recently retired from her "day job" and is now devoting herself to writing. She has completed her second novel and is now doing the hard part—selling it. A portion of her remaining time is spent as a member of a semiprofessional dance company, composed of women much younger than herself. The company dances approximately twenty performances a year, with four hours of rehearsal each week. At sixty-six, she is the crone of the group. One dance in the company's repertoire features her as a crone teaching tribal dances to a little girl. She loves life, wants to change the common image of "older women," and does that with daily workouts, dancing, and tending six acres with her husband, Ted.

Dancer in the Mirror

Age is like darkness on a summer night when you're outside playing Kick-the-Can. You're so involved in the game you don't realize what's happening around you until the can gets lost in the shadows. That's when you look up, see lights clicking on in houses, hear mothers shouting, "Right now or else," and realize it's dark.

My friend Kara has fewer gray hairs than I. Actually, she's lived fewer years. But we fit together. Recently we sipped a Monday morning cup of tea and nibbled on the idea of sneaky aging.

"The shadows of age are so gradual at the beginning," I said. "For me it wasn't the first few gray streaks. Those were "premature." It wasn't even the laugh lines around the eyes. I blamed those on tracks left by good jokes and bright sun. Know what I mean?"

"Sure," Kara said. "A few spider veins appear and it's not aging, it's just kid number two and the extra thirty pounds it took to get him here. Right?"

"Right!"

We sipped in silence.

"But." Kara stirred more milk into her cup. "Does getting older have to mean an end to life as we know it? She thought about that for a minute. "Could be fun. 'Sides, we're not alone in this. There's a whole group of women stepping onto this new road with us."

New road. But why had I noticed no street signs? No flashing lights? Mapless, I'd somehow left the familiar old freeway and made a turn. The hot flashes didn't even signal the switch. There are great jokes to see you through those, plus the company of many other women dosing up on "Pro and Prem" for myriad reasons, not all of them related to growing old. For me it was almost as though I woke up one morning to find age there in bed with me, in places it had never been before. Like when the right shoulder developed a bit of bursitis, which comes and goes, hurting in the morning most of all. Or the night I was reading the newspaper in bed and glanced up to see the skin on my forearm draping in little folds. "No! There's been a mistake. It's not time yet," I yelped. (My mate pulled his attention from Jay Leno and said, "What are you talking about? I haven't moved a muscle." But that's another story.)

Until recent years, age was always the permanent status of my parents. It never occurred to me that they once played Kick-the-Can in broad daylight, before shadows began to drift down from the eaves.

"Ever heard of the Crone thing?" Kara asked, as the artist in her drove her to fold the cloth napkin into a fan pattern.

"Crone thing?" I made a face at the thought. "That sounds old and shriveled."

"It's supposed to sound wise. Crones are, you know, the keepers of the clan wisdom; the teachers of the tribal dances."

I liked the tribal dance idea. Kara and I are both in a dance company. Our love of dance is another joy that makes us fit together so well. Our weekly routines revolve around four-hour Monday-night rehearsals. A note from one's doctor or undertaker is the only acceptable excuse for absence.

As the technique level of the company has increased, I've come to accept the fact that I am not a principal dancer. It's not the age, I tell myself, it's just that others have had more training. I wonder if I, being the oldest in the company, am perhaps the token Crone and haven't realized it. It does feel a bit lonely sometimes, being fifteen or twenty years older than the other women in the group. Not that any of the others try to make me feel that way.

"It's pretty tribal, what we do," Kara said. "Most of our dances are spiritual in nature."

"Yeah," I said, my mind roaming over past performances. "Peace and justice themes, eclectic music, New Age, jazz, rock, hymns."

"I mean how much more 'tribal' can you get," Kara adds, "than dancing at rituals like worship services, baptisms, memorial services, weddings? I mean, it's not like we just do concerts."

"Oh, and Kara, I just remembered the *Hecatomb* dance. I guess I was dancing the Crone part. I just didn't know the term. And I'm still not sure I like it."

"Oh, yeah, where you taught Carrie's little girl about herbs and flowers and tribal steps. See there? You're an experienced Crone. And

I probably shouldn't tell you this, but I think a black crow is the symbol for Crones."

"A crow? That's awful! Who wants to be an old black crow? Why not a dove or butterfly or panther? Anything but a crow."

Kara smiled.

"And," I said, "I not only didn't have any grand solo dance part in *Hecatomb*, I got burned at the stake! Oh, well." We both chuckled. "How do you know about these Crones? You haven't experienced your first night sweats yet."

"I read about it somewhere. Groups of women, over fifty I think, come together and determine to remain active and involved and outrageous."

Outrageous. I did like that idea.

"It's taking the new road, but doing it together."

"Guess I never thought about a group of women joining up to wither together. Be different from the old college dorm crowd, or the group of lactating ladies who stayed together after birthing classes. Maybe not as intimidating as the Lycra-clad hard-bodies at the gym."

"But that's the point. It's not group support for withering, it's group support for proving there's more to getting older than not looking like Bo Derek. Might check it out."

We parted. Kara left these thoughts for me beside her empty teacup.

I went back to the computer keyboard and let the writer's block thing take over. My thoughts wandered. *Face it. My body has been giving me some strong hints for some time now that things are changing. The body knows. It's the mind that's so reluctant to accept the phenomenon of aging.*

Mostly I've seen myself as a contemporary of the other women in the dance company. I admit they memorize much faster, but it infuriates me to suspect that they attribute my slow brain to aging. I have had no memory most of my life, and I'm proud of it! I was born without memory the way some people are born without dimples. It's not because of age that I keep asking "right foot?" or "left foot?"

When I tell someone I dance, invariably they say, "Oh, do you teach?"

"No, damnit!" I'm tempted to shout. "I perform—just like a real, live person."

Until I retired from my day job a few months ago, I saw myself as the equal of my coworkers at the office, even though most of them are under forty and I am s-s-sixt . . . much older! The under-forties assumed that because they thought of me as old, I thought of me as old. A call came for me at the office not long before I left. Young, wrinkle-free Jane answered and called to young, wrinkle-free Carol, "Some woman is on the phone saying she's BJ's mother-in-law. Her mother-in-law is still living?"

Society is my mirror. From all angles, I get shocking and unexpected reminders of my changing status. Last week I was sitting at a stoplight when a white-haired man in the lane to my right looked my way and smiled and winked. I looked to my left. No elderly type there. What was that old codger thinking. It must have been a particularly bad hair day, because later—and let it here be noted that it was after dark—at the Dairy Queen drive-up window, the little snippet of a clerk asked if I'd like to take advantage of their senior discount. All right, so last summer's freckles haven't faded from the backs of my hands. Doesn't mean I'm a *senior*, for heaven's sake!

I continue to work out, to stay on top of the meaning of important terms like "dot-com," "Smashing Pumpkins," and "way cool." I have a cell phone so tiny it sometimes gets lost in my ear. I know what a "Boardhead" bumper sticker means. I am getting older, but am I ready for Cronedom?

Maybe Kara is right. Flying with the Crones could be fun, I guess. I mean, it would be a whole new experience. A flight pattern free of birth-control worries, free of the frantic chauffeuring of kids from point A to point B. And one's perspective does change with the years. I wasn't even interested in Monica's lipstick color when watching her chat with Barbara. I cherish my nook in life, filled with favorite books and favorite paintings and favorite animals. Achieving Crone status is perhaps "a good thing," as our Diva of Doilies might say. Flying with a flock of similarly feathered friends could be a whole new exciting experience. Besides, I've always looked best in black.

Age is just another stage of the life experience. Right? I could learn to like this new me. Is it all right if I still like me better with a little help from my LizSports and the sixty-dollar highlighting job by Mr. Michael? I need to admit that maybe I'm *nearing* what some people might refer to as middle age. OK, "older middle age." I have no objection to the aging process. I respect my elders, when I can find some. Most people grow in wisdom and graciousness as they age. It's just that I haven't fully accepted that I am among them yet.

It was right after that I threw on my way-cool sweats and cross-trainers and headed for Safeway to lay in a supply of food. A little broccoli here, a few apples there—nothing in those choices to say I'm old. I inventoried the contents of my shopping cart: no Depends, no Metamucil, no Grecian Formula.

But there *was* that tiny can of Crisco.

A little dollop of shortening like that, in earlier years, wouldn't have lasted the family a week. Cupcakes, pies, cookies, fish. But now the birdlets have built their own nests, returning only for holidays, childcare, short-term loans, and engine repair. My husband and I eat out. We meet after work for a glass of wine, a bit of pasta; we leave someone else to do the dishes, and we pay with *his* senior discount card. When I do cook, I don't bake room treats or even pies much anymore. We've gone to faux-fat sprays and olive oil. Low-cholesterol stuff. We've certainly taken new avenues in our eating habits.

Yet it could be fun to have aging women friends to be outrageous with, others experiencing this new phase.

I just checked with Mr. Webster. He says a crone is "a withered old woman." He could be wrong. It could be the wrinkles are symbols, badges even. The way I see it, each represents a laugh, a ray of sunshine, a sorrow, or a worry that etched strength and character into the soul. And the silver hairs are a collection of memories. Memories of holding one's breath as a child stutters through the lines of her first play. Or of waiting for the return of a teen out past curfew, while sirens wail in the distance. Of tight budgets and high fevers, marital spats and dandelions. Not all memories can be neatly pasted into scrapbooks. Some of them we wear like road maps of where we've been.

Think I'll take flight with the Crones. But crows? Do they have to be crows? Wait for me, way-cool flock. Let me kick that can. But first, has anyone seen my glasses?

FAN BENNO-CARIS

*Fan Benno-Caris is a world-class athlete who has won more than
fifty medals in national and international racewalking events.
A racewalker since the age of seventy, she also keeps her ninety-
eight-pound frame trim with three- to six-mile walks, ballet and
self-defense classes, and a weight-lifting schedule. In addition to
her physical achievements, she has also been an intuitive counselor
for thirty-five years. Some clients have the opportunity to share both
these aspects of Fan's life as she counsels them while training on the
track. Fan is a sought-after motivational speaker, and has been
featured in a commercial and in various magazines. She carries a
special dictionary from which she has cut out the word "exercise,"
because she prefers to just say "move!"*

Walking My Talk at Eighty-Two

As an octogenarian, I live life actively, fulfilling many roles. I'm a wife, mother, grandmother, great-grandmother, and friend. I am an intuitive counselor, working professionally with people of all ages. And each day before the sun goes down, I train for one to two hours—on the roads, the track, and in the gym. You see, in addition to everything else I do, I'm a competitive racewalker.

Sometimes I think younger people become so busy growing up that they think it unimportant to talk to those of us who have walked their similar paths. Perhaps they think we have little or nothing beneficial to share. Perhaps they think they know more than we do. Or perhaps they fear looking directly into the eyes and minds of elders, even though many of us are living and aging actively.

People from around the globe call and talk to me about their lives, about mine, and about life in general. They are curious to hear how I've gotten to where I am today—racewalking from one adventure to the next. It's almost as if living to be professionally and athletically active at eighty-plus years is somehow beyond their comprehension. I suppose that to many, it is. The fact is, as they continue to grow and develop toward my age, I've already "been" every one of their years. To me, life is one gigantic jigsaw puzzle, and we are each responsible for putting it together in our unique way. That is the most interesting and intriguing thing about life. Ultimately, as we finish one puzzle, we either add a new piece or start the challenge of piecing together a brand-new one from scratch. That, I believe, is what makes a life of difference.

I believe it's my responsibility, even my legacy, to share my wisdom with others. If growing older while living young is to be my legacy, then the most important lesson I can teach people of all ages is to get *moving!* Whether through my work or just by being the person I am, I feel that I can help others learn how to help themselves. When they walk with me, I can show them ways by which they can make anything happen. I should know. I've learned a thing or two when it comes to turning life's risks into rewards and blessings.

You need only walk a short distance with me to believe that life is for the living. If that sounds strange, it isn't. Every day, I counsel people on various topics concerning work, family, love, finances, and more. Surprisingly, no matter what their age, many of the people I counsel view life through worn-out lenses, counting life in years gone by—or, more frightening, they continue to live past experiences over and over again. My work is to get them to take what they know, and add to the puzzle—to move on to new and adventurous journeys.

Pablo Picasso said, "It takes a long time to become young." This hasn't been hard for me to achieve, because I've lived young all my life. Those close to me contend that I have a tremendous capacity for love, compassion, loyalty, and trust. I suppose I come by these qualities naturally; they were given me by two very loving and compassionate people—my father and mother. They taught me to believe that deep within our psyche is a pilot light that can ignite a great sense of purpose and passion for living a treasured life. I am who I am, and I do what I do today, because of this cherished philosophy.

When I was seventeen, I dreamed of moving to New York City to become a dancer; but I moved instead to the nearby bustling city of Dallas, where I met and married a banker, had three children, and managed to sandwich sixty-three years of challenges and rewards in between then and now.

The extent of my "sporting" life was dancing when I was young. Later, I taught others to dance. I didn't run. I didn't swim. I had some fears about water, which I learned to overcome when I was sixty. Learning to swim opened up the floodgates, so to speak, to many new opportunities. I later learned that I was in very good company in overcoming such obstacles. Eleanor Roosevelt had herself shared such a fear, and only after having children did she venture into a water world. When asked why, she stated simply and directly that because her children went into areas she feared to go, she had no choice but to learn if she was to follow them. You could say that we both transformed our own unique jigsaw puzzles by not only looking directly into the eyes of fear, but by taking action!

Great teachers are disguised in life experiences. You see, Eleanor Roosevelt and I shared a FEAR, or False Expectation of Assumed

Realities. I had assumed there was something real to fear about the water, yet the fear itself was simply in the perception that water had control over me. When I reframed that thought and realized that it was I who had finally taken control of my choices, I experienced the joy of swimming in the pool with my grandchildren. You see, we all become swimmers in our way, when we take the plunge!

I added a new piece to my already multidimensional jigsaw puzzle when I turned seventy. What an inspired puzzle it has become since I became a competitive athlete! Had I not attended that one special seminar held at the Cooper Aerobic Center in Dallas, I would never have thought to don a T-shirt with a racing number pinned to the front, step onto a track, and compete against like-minded octogenarians, all going for the Gold. When the speaker, an Olympic racewalker, completed his talk, I boldly walked up to him and announced my intent to win at the World Games! He grinned, thinking I was kidding, but realized only milliseconds later that I was indeed very serious, when I said again, "Tell me what I need to do. I'm anxious to get started!" He respectfully outlined the steps I would need to take to qualify in all divisions of city, state, national, and, finally, international levels. Little did he know that a decade later I would be ranked second in the world in my age division, and be named "Racewalker of the Year, 1999," along with receiving many other awards. I am quite literally racewalking through everything I do.

As I find myself flying around the world, competing against others in my division and with people of all ages and professions, I'm continually interviewed for newspaper and magazine articles, and television and radio segments on the topic of what keeps me so young and active. I speak to various groups, associations, clubs, hospitals, independent-living facilities, and more. What piques the audiences' curiosity is what I'm doing at my age! I simply tell them, "Look, I just forgot to get older." On some level I absolutely understand their astonishment, especially when they realize what I'm doing at my age: competing in athletic events, counseling others, spending time with family and friends, and traveling the world. Honestly, I don't even think about my calendar age until someone else brings it up. Then it's almost as startling to me as it is intriguing to them. Quite frankly, I don't know what age is supposed to look like. What I do know is that the key to living young is to stay consistently active and busy.

Several years ago, I was invited to speak to a young and energetic group of graduate students in a gerontology class at the University of Colorado about how someone like me gets to be at the top of her game. I couldn't help noticing the students' wide-eyed attention as I spoke, and, in my typical manner, modeled my racewalking techniques. I like to keep moving from one side of the stage to the other, especially when speaking before crowds of any size.

As I continued to speak, it was if another had suddenly taken control of my thoughts. I confronted these young students with the question, "When you're my age, what will you be doing?" The hush in the room was nearly earsplitting. There they sat, innocent young twenty-somethings, listening to one of the women they've been taught to categorize within a "geriatric" population. A woman they normally would define as "fragile, becoming mentally and physically challenged with age." But actually someone with whom, on their best days, they would have a difficult time keeping in step with, and who sounded and acted younger than they and most of their twenty-something friends.

Kenneth Cooper, M.D., known internationally as "the father of aerobics," once referred to me as the role model for what aging should look like. I've lived through eleven presidents' administrations, several wars, and a host of global events. Yet, in this world where anything is possible, I'm living not in a fragile, diminished mental and physical state (where these soon-to-be gerontologists might academically pigeonhole me), but as an active woman who doesn't feel a day over thirty-five.

My focus is on eating healthy foods, exercising, forming new relationships, maintaining those I've cultivated through the years, ensuring that my husband, children, grandchildren and great-grandchildren are healthy and happy, and interacting effectively with my clients—along with all of the other aspects that make my life rewarding. The degree of my mental, emotional, and physical endurance, and my flexibility and strength, comes from the ways in which I, like a sponge, continually absorb and put all my life's lessons into play.

Others make their own choices. We all engage in this very important life competition; how we deal with what happens during the event, and how far a distance we are willing to travel, is what makes all the difference. Why live any other way?

Sport, a form of perpetual play, gives meaning to everything else in life, adding many dimensions to what we are and what we can become. It has helped me keep perspective in all that I do, like playing with my granddaughter, running around the malls during the holiday seasons, traveling around the world and into different time zones while adjusting my physiology to compete. I wish I had been active in this way when I was in my thirties. Yet, what is most important—I'm living this way now, in my eighties! Sport has given me a different way to view my world, and made me more productive than ever.

I recall my grandson's response when a newspaper reporter once asked him about my athletic prowess. He said, "One grandmother bakes cookies and the other one lifts weights!"

My zest for living has only increased over the years. I now speak publicly on the topic of how you can successfully work toward finding your life's purpose and passion. Recently, I was asked to open up a new walking path in the city of Addison, a suburb of Dallas. The mayor, himself a walker, is negotiating with me to create a walking club and teach walking classes to people of all ages in this rapidly growing community. This may be yet another way in which I can teach people to add new puzzle pieces to their already gigantic jigsaw puzzles—and make them fit.

I have taken executive speaking classes, to help me feel more comfortable in front of all the groups who frequently schedule my appearances. I was asked to speak to a group of young junior-college students. I was told there would be fifteen, maybe twenty students. When I arrived, the gym was packed with people, with little room for me to show them my racewalking techniques! I can speak to all ages, because I have no age. Everyone wants to learn how to walk, how to grow older while living young, how to be positive and active.

I continue to compete in racewalking, and I've recently added a new piece to my sports puzzle. I'm currently learning the art of self-defense. Until recently, I had no knowledge of how to protect myself if ever I found myself in a situation where I needed to do so. I signed up, and guess what? I fell in love with a sport all over again! I want to work toward earning my Black Belt! When I recently made that announcement to my instructor, he responded with a grin similar to the Olympic racewalker's of nearly a decade ago. If he only knew that story, he wouldn't have said, "Not in this lifetime, you won't!" He doesn't know me very well. I committed to my instructor when I answered him, "Well, at least I can try." Stay tuned.

If someone had told me many yesterdays ago that someday in my eighties, a character in an upcoming Hollywood screenplay would be based on me, or that I'd be competing as an athlete, making television commercials, and being invited onto national talk shows, I would not have believed them. In my youth, I dreamed of becoming a world-renowned dancer. Today, I'm an international racewalker who rumbas from one competition to the next. I have focus, determination, and the all-important discipline and persistence that enables me to effectively face any challenge. I am today the culmination of all my past and present experiences.

I'm excited by my opportunities to debunk the many myths of aging. Being an active role model allows me to help others make changes in their lives, to help them develop new ways to look at their old ways. This is what's most exciting to me; this is what I do best.

We are each responsible for putting together our own unique puzzle. I'm a ninety-eight-pound woman who has lived a little. With the moxie to continually add new pieces to my own gigantic life puzzle, I'm having the time of my life. I don't know what my puzzle will look like when it's finished—I'll be too busy creating a new one somewhere else. All I can say is that as you continue to enhance your jigsaw puzzle, remember that the fun is realized in piecing it together. Do I harbor aspirations for the future, after winning more than fifty different medals, trophies, and ribbons? Of course! I plan to win the World Games eighteen years from now. I'll be one hundred years young, and I invite all of you to be there.

SARAH BIERMANN

*Sarah Biermann was born in Michigan in 1945, and grew up
in New Jersey, Illinois, and Kentucky. She earned her B.A. and
began graduate classes in education at the University of Iowa.
Family has always been her first priority, followed by various
jobs in the fields of education and seasonal work. She spends
her free time with friends, reading, gardening, enjoying
nature, working on projects with her husband, Jim,
playing flute, and writing poetry.*

Like an Old Tree

The tree in my front yard stands strong and tall; deep roots anchor it against the winds. Its age is readily recognized by its thick, dark, ragged bark. Although it leans slightly to the north, it has withstood many violent storms. Green, velvety moss allows it to blend in with its skirt of hostas. Its umbrella-like branches once shaded a wooden swing, now gone. Sitting beside the tree, I recall the days when two little girls in bunny slippers and nightgowns ran beneath and around it as the sun set in the Midwestern sky. Now I look again at its skin: such deep furrows and beautiful lines. In my eyes, I am that tree.

Could it be that the wisdom of older women can be measured by their wrinkles, as the tree's growth is measured by its rings? I am proud of my wrinkles—wrinkles that mirror the years of my youth, that release laughter and tears, that leak worry and sorrow, that reflect that I was a teacher, a mother, a daughter, an aunt, a granddaughter, a homemaker, a gardener, a builder, a bookkeeper, and a cook. Oh, my! I envision myself getting fatter and fatter with each new ring! My tree's rings speak, too—of the many rains that gave its branches new growth, of the yearly snowstorms that gave nourishment to the roots that grow deep into the hillside, and of the much-needed warmth of the life-giving sun.

As I have aged, I've noticed how my rings have increased in number. My daughter loves to tease me by feeling the flab at my elbow, or by gently nudging the ring around my midriff. My appearance may be changing, but my life is still precious. I believe that as I age and wander, I become more valuable to those around me. I feel that I can share my stumbling and not look backward—but, like the tree, reach for the sun, growing toward the upward and onward. I look to the women in my community. Some look up to us as mentors, as experienced mothers, as wanna-be therapists with wisdom concerning the majors and minors of parenting. Others look to us for empathy as they return to college for that long-awaited education. Older women will always keep growing wrinkles in the gray matter.

Inside the house, at the top of the stairs, is another tree, this one long dead—a walnut tree now in the shape of a small chest. Its age is recognized by the ornate knobs of old—black wooden drops that dangle from metal hinges—and the three drawers with etched designs. It has a curved backboard, and a piece of glass adorns its top surface, which holds an antique globe lamp. The chest is full of lace-edged linens that have been passed down through the generations. It is truly unique.

The same holds true for my friends, each one with her own special personality and "lines," and each one of whom holds the wisdom obtained from years of life experiences. I like to think of us as "antiques in progress," our value increasing with our age. The furrows of our brows, the crow's-feet around our eyes, the smile lines around our mouths, the folds of our necks, all show our worth. A person can try to polish us, get rid of the blemishes, repair us, give us new parts, but we are priceless just the way we are. My peers notice my bifocals, my old-age spots, my matronly abdomen, and the soft pads on my hipbones, but they accept me for my understanding and companionship. I look to them for the same. Perhaps that is what each year has taught us: inner contentment is of more value than polished, sleek surfaces. The tree, the chest, and the women: all are aging, a little worn, yet priceless.

As I grow older, I seek out women who still challenge their skills. They must have an inner yearning to learn and seek knowledge. Then, they must be willing to share that wisdom in turn. It doesn't matter if it comes from a formal group or just a small group like the Friends of the Library here in our small town. I have always been blessed with wise women in my life. I think of them when I see the top of that old tree in my yard stretching far into the sky, indicating a wide root system underground. Their family roots, spiritual values, strong work ethic, yards full of flowers, love of literature, and sense of community define these women. Each has her own "rings" of life—her own antique quality, where thoughts of sentimental objects abound.

My community of women is like a grove of walnut trees, or an antique shop where the variety and age of each item increases every year. It is a place where we women still encourage one another as our nests empty and we grow our gray hairs. It is wonderful to be getting older here. I am proud of my wrinkles, my crow's-feet, and the stretch marks on my belly. My friends feel the same way. Perhaps in the decade ahead, as we retire from our careers, we will find ourselves sitting under my tree with our needlepoint, our counted cross-stitch, our coffee, and new bits of wisdom. Now, as I watch the sun set in the west through the big, strong branches of my tree, I know that I have had a full, blessed life—rings, wrinkles, and all.

YVONNE MOKIHANA CALIZAR

Yvonne Mokihana Calizar is a writer and teacher living in
Kuli'ou'ou Valley, on the Eastside of O'ahu, Hawai'i. She has lived
and worked in Washington State, and has shared her skills and
expertise with colleges, corporations and community groups
throughout the Pacific Northwest and Hawai'i. Her work as teacher
and writer fosters creativity, personal growth, widening of
perspectives, and multicultural sensitivity, and integrates Hawaiian
culture and language. Calizar has written and published several
books, a collection of poetry, and magazine articles. She writes a
regular column called Makua o'o for the Hawaii Island Journal.
Portions of her essay have appeared in Ka'u Landing Magazine and
Grace Magazine. Her Web site is www.hellomyheart.com.

Nana I Ke Ku...
Looking to the Source

I don't say we're old, but some say it. "We're at that age," they say. What age is that, anyway? Middle age, half-moon age. When old friends gather and widen the circle of stones to include their daughters, the question of age becomes a fuller story. The wisdom of having lived stretches the limits of younger expectations. Things from the "sometime in my life I'm gonna" list becomes "what's happening now."

I laugh as Michele and I drive off in her rental Mustang, waving to Nola's only child. She peeks out through the opened louvers of her tiny cottage and giggles at us. "That looks so cool." It's not as though one ride in a red Mustang convertible turns this pair of *Pake*-Hawaiian *wahine* into candidates for the Thelma and Louise gallery. But it does give us both memories of another great time together, doing stuff that we could not create separately.

Living from the middle has something to do with being able to see life's beginning and end. We have gathered to shower our daughters with aunty-wisdom—drinking tea and sips of wine as we prepare a young woman for marriage—and to celebrate birthdays with friends who are living with diseases known to take lives. We have lived long enough to understand the meaning and value of wandering, and we live the lesson of needing to explore the world without forgetting who we were in the beginning. Each of us has danced the movements of *auana* and wandered far from the home place, where a backyard sock-baseball diamond was a giants' field, requiring many strides to reach second base.

Some days pass like racing clouds in front of a nearly full moon. The shape and luster of the clouds shift without asking, and delight pairs of human eyes as we watch how quickly the skyscape changes. Seated on the smooth caramel-colored slats of the worn teak bench, a childhood companion joins me in the sharing of one of those times, when clouds race, and moonbeams play. Forty years earlier, this friend and I spent time in this same backyard, and played in the shadows of the trees. In the shade of mango boughs, we spent time together in places bound in the magic syrup of children's imaginations. We did things without organization. Our parents didn't watch; they left us to our world. In the process, memories were created to be shared again and again in seamless film between *ke`ia* and *kela*. *Ke`ia*, now. *Kela*, over there.

Five years ago I returned to Kuli`ou`ou Valley on the island of O`ahu. More than twenty years away from the homeplace had changed me. I had adapted to life in a small, white, middle-class community in Washington State. Through the years, I chose to tuck my Hawaiian spirit tightly away in a *pu`olo* bundle, and only shared it sparingly. To be "myself" out loud would have been too much.

Instead, I bottled up most of the longings for home, and grafted a new form of being onto my original stock of twenty-four-year-old growth. On the outside, I learned to wear layers of long underwear to keep me warm. Although we raised our son along the shores of beautiful Puget Sound, I can count on two hands the number of times I swam in this nearly salty, rarely warm water. My body allowed layers of silk, polyester and cotton to surround me when the cool days of fall turned to winter cold. But this woman of warm Pacific saltwater never forgot the feel of Waimanalo Beach water—the temperature of my mother's womb, the texture and enveloping comfort unmatched. It was this water and the wind *ka makani* that always called.

Divorce poked *puka*, holes, in that *puòlo*, and my spirit began to flow from the tightly bound container. It was a messy sight, that ooze. My mother raised me to be loyal. Ma's steadfast jaw and lifelong mantra "never change horses in midstream" became part of my condition. Genetics gave me the jaw. The mantra was an old melody I lived without questioning, until Roy told me he wanted a divorce. I still hear our son Christopher telling us, "I can accept that, but it will take time for me to understand it." Ahhh. The tall, lacy fingers of cedar soothed me as healing salves do, and slowly allowed me to begin re-dreaming myself, gathering up my oozing spirit into something yet to be. The wind inside me knew it was time to go home and make peace with the *puka* and move with my spirit flow. *Ka Makani*—the wind outside—reminded me that a journey of migration meanders, and her movements carry no judgment.

When a woman remakes herself, as she must do many times while in the body, the skills of navigating and translating are called upon without thinking. If we are to move with the water, as people of the canoe, we must be able to read the way. Signs, shifts, and nature's messages are often subtle, and translating them accurately takes practice. Living as island people on a postage-stamp piece of earth surrounded by ocean is humbling. There is a balance and a promise that is our birthright. Live only on the white part of the stamp, on the edges. *Malama*, care for, the middle, because the land will continue to feed you. Forget that, and the stamp shrinks.

Ka Makani, the shape-shifting wind, blew me home. The moments, minutes, days and weeks of being back where I began have allowed me to experience what Natalie Goldberg calls "wild mind." The *puka* made by divorce are no longer the enemy. They are instead tiny portals pecked in my grafted self at forty-six, as escape hatches, openings to this wild mind. Without them, my spirit might have remained contained, root-bound, restless and fermenting. In the culture of my mother's people, they would say I was finally *Nana I Ke Kumu*, looking to the source.

The people of old say that the wind carries with her everything and everybody that ever was, and stirs with it all that is now—on the way to becoming everything that might be. Nature has always been a broad mirror that island people view without having to look. This morning the wind is gentle, but strong enough to send the bamboo-anchored paper screens into their click-clank, click-clank wind dance against the front window. The yama bells dangling outside are quiet. I wake before the sun brightens Kuliʻouʻou's dark sides from a deep and delicious night of sleep. Pete stirs beside me and I remember it is Monday morning. A travel day.

Sweethearts and friendships at fifty-two include expanded definitions for being. My long and lanky partner and companion works with
his brother on Maui. The two men are creating a welding and metal
fabricating shop in Kahului, the Maui town where airplanes land and
take off like the commuter ferries in Washington, loaded with folks
who live in one place and work in another. The style of living that
includes commuter relationships is one born from my time of shape-
shifting. This two-island kind of life gives me more time to know who
I am alone.

Being alone without being lonely is a different thing for me. No
marriage. No children. No job. The absence of all three has meant
getting to know what and who I am before I relate to a partner, a
child, or society's expectations. Coming home to hear myself means
being courageous. It's not so much about being strong or moving fast
anymore. I know I can be strong when I must, and accept that I'd
rather not move quite as fast as I used to. I know the route, remember
the clamber. Being courageous means being committed and prepared
to be alone sometimes. At this point, I have made peace with the
puka, the holes within me, and have replaced strength and speed with
discernment and progress. Believing that "simple" works has meant
accepting and celebrating my choices.

My parents created a life for me that worked during the years
when familiar faces shared gentle, regular conversations, and yards
were without squeeching gates and head-high fences. There are times
now when the sounds of gas-powered chainsaws, leaf-blowers, lawn-
mowers, and weed-whackers raise the decibel levels to a chaotic
frenzy, torturing my ears and nervous system. So, I push my reel

mower and feel a small but smiling voice inside saying, "Yah." While doing my taxes, my accountant says, "You are in the lowest income bracket. It takes courage to do that." I look across his boomerang-shaped table and nod. "Life is short," is all I say.

One of the decisions I made at fifty was to invest in myself now. My retirement funds, chocked away years ago when I worked full-time and at full speed, are a major source of income for me now. The simplified living I practice from this Kuli'ou'ou Valley home place, one day at a time, is simple but not always easy.

The hedges of mock orange that are everywhere in this valley are potent and pollen-packed. They send bees into a stupor, and folks like me, with allergies to their fragrance, into temporary refuge. After many years away from these hedges, I have learned that too much of a sweet thing can be just that. Too much! It's part of that discernment training that a *makua o'o*, a maturing adult, must commit to as the body becomes less young, and as the systems within the *kino* lose their capacity to resist assault from pollens, free radicals, or aging attitudes like "controlling the world." It's funny how a hedgeful of tiny blossoms stimulates a new set of capacities for survival. Slowly, strength builds from the inside, and a life I stitch together moment to moment becomes new skin. Gratitude for small miracles and the grace to accept the perfection of an imperfect world fill the *puka* of a once-rigid view of how to be. My bank account breathes because there is so much space there. Open to the potential of "wild mind," I write because that's what I love. These years lived from the middle require more rest, and a gentle but courageous commitment to be a mountain, as I train to be a yoga teacher at fifty-two, and drink tea instead of a soda.

It matters less that others agree with me than it matters that I choose. Slowly—because that's the way nature works, slow to medium—I remember that my birthright is to live on the edge of the postage stamp, and to *malama*, care, for the middle. I choose to be a *Makuahine o'o*, a maturing adult woman living gently on the earth, paying loving attention to the details of nature in the belief that I am part of a grander plan. *Nana I Ke Kumu*. I look to the Source.

SALLY FISHER

Sally Fisher is an author, activist, lecturer, and founder of both Northern Lights Alternatives, an international network of AIDS organizations, and the AIDS Mastery Workshop, which is presented in over thirty cities worldwide. She was Co-Producer of V-DAY 1998, *a star-driven production of Eve Ensler's Obie Award–winning play,* The Vagina Monologues, *in New York City, which raised awareness about violence against women and funds to support organizations involved in ending the violence. Fisher has been involved in producing events for V-DAY, from the Kennedy Center in Washington, DC, to cities as diverse as London and Santa Fe. She is a Producer of V-DAY 2001 to be held at Madison Square Garden, Associate Producer of the Off-Broadway production of* The Vagina Monologues, *and will be involved in the production of Ms. Ensler's* Necessary Targets. *Sally's first book is titled* Life Mastery, *and she has created a series of audiotapes on Spirituality and Burnout. All of her work supports the premise that "The Quality of Life is not determined by the circumstances but by what we do with them," which is the title of her newest book.*

My Eccentric Womanself

A brilliant photographer friend was mounting an exhibition dubbed "Originals," and asked me to be part of it. All of the photographs are of women over forty, most over fifty. They show us in our full flower, full power, and filled with wisdom and sass. As I looked at prints of my image, I was amazed at how much I loved what I saw. Sure, there were some lines, but I've earned them. I've lived them. I saw my character displayed in my bone structure and in the compassion in my eyes. Suddenly I was struck by the fact that, with the exception of a few moments of panic, aging had happened almost without my noticing.

The moments of panic had nothing to do with the milestones in my own life. The first twinge happened when my son, the oldest of my three children, turned thirty. Surely I wasn't old enough to have a kid who was thirty! I was barely past thirty myself! And it happened again when my youngest turned thirty. How could it be? It seemed no time had passed at all. But for the most part, aging has been a graceful proposition.

I had a great role model for aging: my great-aunt. She was called Nennie, which was how the kids in the family pronounced "Edna." She was also the person who came closest to mothering me. Nennie and my great-uncle were childless—her word, not mine—and I was their favorite grand-whatever. I got to spend hours and hours with them. Nennie outlived my great-uncle by many years. She spent her last years in a lovely apartment hotel with a sweeping veranda in the front. I remember that when I would pick her up to go to the symphony or shopping or out for lunch and a martini, she'd look at the other women and the men on the porch and say, "Just look at all these old people. All they do is sit!" She was ninety-something at the time and filled with vigor and wonder.

There's another reason for my comfortable relationship with my age. For the past sixteen years, I've been working with people with AIDS. I was involved in the theater and entertainment industry, where the epidemic reared its head early and with ferocious consequences. I was teaching, producing, and facilitating workshops on creativity and other workshops on developing a spiritual foundation to support and nurture that creativity. The premise of my work has always been that the quality of our lives is determined not by our circumstances but by what we do with them. Friends, colleagues, and students who were infected asked if I would do a workshop for them. I did. It was a life-altering experience. I said goodbye to life as I'd known it and committed myself to this new work.

I saw people who were facing their mortality decide to live fully for whatever amount of time they had left. And many didn't have much time. But they discovered they could cherish every hour and live as powerfully and passionately as possible. Their lives stood as a testament to the idea that we can have a quality life in the face of any circumstances. Certainly if they could thrive in the face of AIDS, I could stop whining about my petty grievances, and surely I couldn't be thrown by a little thing like aging! They reminded me of the sacredness and fragility of life.

When I turned fifty, friends threw an outrageous party for me, and other friends and family came from all over to celebrate. On the day of my birthday, I ran into someone on the street who asked me if I was upset about turning fifty. I asked her to repeat the question. It had never occurred to me to be upset. For one thing, I had a slew of friends who would have loved to confront such a dilemma, friends who never came close to turning fifty before their lives were taken by some permutation of AIDS. And I was having the time of my life! I was healthy, I was sober, and I looked fantastic; I loved my work, had a book in publication, was dating two fabulous men and flirting with a great woman. No. I was not upset about turning fifty. In fact, I was thrilled.

On turning fifty, I decided that I could declare myself officially eccentric. Until then I had been unusual, peculiar, different, or weird, but not eccentric. Now I could be eccentric. In the same manner, I declared myself wise. I was filled with the wisdom of my years and the wisdom I'd gained through my work. You can know a lot before you're fifty, but wisdom is something that is collected and nurtured from knowledge and experience. It percolates. It brews. It steeps. It's not cerebral. It's not knowing or thinking. It's visceral. Wisdom gestates; it expands, becomes enveloping, inclusive. Like a fig or a pear, it takes time to ripen.

I wish that loving myself as a woman had come as naturally. But I was brought up in the years when a woman had little value unless she had a man; had no real intrinsic value unless she married and had children. There were many subtle ways that society's message was reinforced as I grew up, but my mother's approach wasn't subtle at all. She actually told me that women—or rather, girls—weren't to be trusted. She said they would tell me the wrong thing to say and wear so they could steal my boyfriends. This, from a woman who parted my hair in the middle and pulled it back with barrettes on either side, just as my nose began to grow faster than the rest of my face—put me in midriffs when I was chubby, and claimed to love me. Come to think of it, *she* was a woman, and I didn't trust *her*. I adopted her belief system, and so—without understanding what the words "internalized self-loathing" meant—I became a girl who didn't like girls.

I spent time with girls, and referred to many of them as friends, but I didn't trust them, and preferred the company of guys. When I went away to college it was the same thing. After years of longing to be really popular, suddenly I was. I always had a "serious" boyfriend. My bridge games took place at fraternity houses. My best friends were the male friends of the males I dated. I dropped out of my sorority. I had other things in mind. Marriage. After I got married, I gave up my involvement in many of the political movements that had stirred my passions, and dropped out of art school.

I was acquainted with lots of women whom I called friends, but I couldn't really relate to them. They were on all the right committees, and went to all the right parties, and wore the right designer clothes. I felt estranged from them. The one exception was my real friend

Sandy. She was also an artist. Our husbands were friends, we hung out as couples and vacationed together, and we were pregnant with our first kids together.

As a mother of young children, I also befriended a circle of women who sat with me around the sandbox. We yacked about our husbands or shopping or the kids. I loved these women, and though we had varied interests and passions, we were all in the same boat. We saw each other through birthday parties and measles. It was the first time I thoroughly understood that women weren't out to get me.

But it wasn't until I became involved in the art world and the peace movement that I saw women who were as powerful as the men I knew, and had lives that were entirely their own. Along with Sandy, two other women artists, Andrea and Freya, became my first experience of sisterhood. We acted as sources of inspiration and support for one another in our careers as artists and in our personal lives. We were an outrageous unit that waltzed through the art scene in Chicago, where we all lived at the time.

Andrea and I had a construction company together, which we called "X." When anyone asked us to do anything—paint a room, rebuild a gallery, crate or truck art—we'd say yes. Then we'd have to figure out how to do it. In fact, every time we'd say yes, I'd buy another "how to" book. What we lacked in competence we made up for in sheer will. We were women doing work that was usually considered the stuff "guys" do. We loved our mystique. We came to hate the hard labor.

Our lives took on a sort of sitcom ambience. Once we painted a brand-new condominium with brand-new, shining hardwood floors. I was on top of a very tall ladder with a fresh supply of white paint,

and—you guessed it. One Friday the thirteenth, we had three paintings for delivery tied on top of a car. One flew off on the freeway. But
somehow people kept hiring us, and we kept having the best and
worst of times. We laughed constantly, were completely bonded as sisters, cried a lot, and, it seems to me, spent an inordinate amount of
time soaking in Masada salts.

Andrea, Sandy, Freya and I, magnificent women that we were,
helped each other construct and install our art exhibitions, and got
deeply involved in each other's personal bids for freedom, divorces, and
escapes to New York. As each of us moved, we'd help set the stage for the
next to embrace the lives we knew were waiting for us. These sisters and
other amazing women, who began to appear all over my life, showed me
how fantastic women were. I was a woman, and as a woman I began to
see myself as fantastic as well. It wasn't until my internalized sexism
lifted that I realized it had been there in the first place.

There are no words to express my love for women and how proud
and grateful I am to be a woman. But it was only when I was able to see
the beauty and power of other women that I was able to see my own
beauty and power. I also understand how deeply shamed I had been by
being a woman in a family and a society that told me I wasn't valued.

Sadly, this is the experience of sisters all over the world, many of
whom are persecuted and tortured by their governments and religions.
Some live where they are owned by their fathers and husbands, or where
battery against them is condoned, simply because they are women.
Physical, psychological, emotional, and psychic violence creates an
internalized self-loathing that runs deep to the core of their being.

In the past few years I have been able to bring my life full circle. In addition to my AIDS work, I have returned to the arts. I produce theater and gala events called V-DAY, which raise awareness about violence against women. I work with two brilliant sisters, Eve and Willa, who share a vision of a world where women are safe and can stand tall together. I want all women to be able to live full, rich, passionate, creative lives and to grow old knowing their worth. I want all women to look in the mirror, or at photographs of themselves, with satisfaction and wonder.

I remember the day I first saw *Ms. Magazine* at a newsstand. It was their first-ever issue. I was married at the time, and not exactly thrilled with my circumstances and status as wife and hearthkeeper. I bought the magazine. I brought it home. I looked at the letters: *Ms.* I just kept staring at them. *Ms.* The letters didn't say "Miss" and they didn't say "Mrs." They said "Ms." A little thrill went through my body. That's who I was, *Ms.* Sally Fisher, not *Mrs.* anybody, not the extension of a husband, not just a wife. I went to my desk and gathered up all of the stationery and informal note cards that designated me as a Mrs. I built a fire in the living-room fireplace and burned them all, never to call myself "Mrs." again. I was suddenly so proud to be a woman that I thought I'd burst, and I've never stopped being proud.

And now I'm proud to be a woman over fifty—a woman on the way toward sixty, who spends time among wonderful women of the same "certain age." I am part of a glorious women's group. We began as a group of women over fifty. That was then. This is now. Our concerns have changed and broadened. The level of our intimacy has deepened. We have shared menopause remedies, arthritis miracle cures, our deepest secrets, our sex lives, our hearts' desires, and above all our power and vulnerability.

The artist sisters with whom I shared my days of wild exploration; the women with whom I seek to shift society's view of women; and this women's group, no less wild, with whom I share the days of gathering wisdom—all are an important part of my being. Like fine wine, we get better, richer, and a bit more full-bodied with age. We have a new boldness and a new quality of heart. We stand as great role models for other women.

All of this said, I have discovered a new role model of my own to stand beside my great-aunt. Because of my involvement in AIDS, I frequently read the obituaries. I came upon one that was written in story form about Mary Lou Lollis, who died at 103. She had been a storyteller, among other things. Her obituary spoke of how she had been born in a time without radio, and how she had embraced change.

It also said that though she was never rich, she always did what she could for others. "When hard times came in the Depression, Mrs. Lollis began making pies in her kitchen." Fats Waller dubbed her "The Pie Lady." She did what she could for families devastated by the dive in our nation's economy. She lived in Harlem, where music was in the air. She kept the stories of a happier, healthier time alive for generations to follow. "People of all ages said they learned a lot about twentieth-century history listening to Mrs. Lollis, but it was the children whose eyes would get the widest and who would listen the hardest when Mrs. Lollis stood up and started telling stories about how things were in the old days." She was described as always caring and always willing to be of service. The story also noted that she had to slow down a little when she hit 101.

She lived the fullest of lives and contributed what she was able. What could be more wonderful? To live well, live fully, and know that you've been a wise woman, leaving a legacy of caring. Some women leave large and sweeping legacies, or affect the tide of history. Others are meant to leave a much smaller legacy. It doesn't matter. What matters is that when life comes to an end we are well pleased with our participation. It is a blessing when we can look back and note that we have lived in accordance with our spiritual, political, and personal principles, and that we have contributed to the fullest of our ability to the quality of our own lives and the lives of those we touch.

George Bernard Shaw has stated it exquisitely, in *Man and Superman*:

> This is the true joy in life, the being used for a purpose recognized by yourself as a mighty one; the being a force of nature instead of a feverish selfish little clod of ailments and grievances complaining that the world will not devote itself to making you happy.
>
> I am of the opinion that my life belongs to the whole community and, as long as I live, it is my privilege to do for it whatever I can.
>
> I want to be thoroughly used up when I die, for the harder I work, the more I live. I rejoice in life for its own sake. Life is no "brief candle" to me. It is a sort of splendid torch which I have got hold of for the moment, and I want to make it burn as brightly as possible before handing it on to future generations.

ANTHEA FRANCINE

Anthea Francine is a Certified Professional Personal Coach and has given workshops, taught classes, coached individuals and couples, created rituals, and celebrated rites of passage in many spiritual, health, education, and personal growth–oriented organizations. Her credentials include an M.A. in Theology and the Arts from the Pacific School of Religion; a B.A. in Social Welfare and Psychology from UC Berkeley; a Certificate in Organizational Development and Transformation from the California Institute of Integral Studies; and additional certificates in leadership arts, communication skills, and Native American wisdom traditions. With her holistic approach to spiritual traditions and bodywork, Anthea is dedicated to restoring our ancient commitment to living an authentic, balanced, and compassionate life.

Questions of Aging

The question of aging looms very large on my personal horizon at this time. A week ago I spent my fifty-fifth birthday in England (where I was born, and where I grew up) with my mother, who celebrated her eighty-fifth birthday just four days later. This year I really feel as if I am standing on the line between middle age and "aging." Thinking back over my life, I realize that this transition is as potent as every transition between life cycles has been for me—not only because my life work is to ponder the deeper questions, but also because I belong to a generation of women who are pioneers. We have been consciously searching for and bringing back feminine values since we were in our teens—and speaking for myself, I can say that I was doing it even as a child, without the language to express my internal struggles and longings!

In my early twenties I was deeply aware, as a young married woman, that a woman's story and meaning finished mythologically in our culture with the last sentence of the popular fairytales of the time:

and they lived happily ever after. . . . Married in Zurich, Switzerland, at twenty-two, still childless and very unhappy in my relationship at twenty-seven, I was profoundly aware that this was not to be the case in my life. Searching for some kind of reliable guidance outside the cultural authorities of church and state, in the mid-sixties I came across the work of Carl Jung. My dreams became my guides and wisdom source, and it was there that I first met the manifestation of the nurturing masculine and feminine (*animus* and *anima*) within myself, and became deeply aware that we are each unique and precious Souls who need to be unconditionally cared for in mind, body, spirit, and soul in order to fulfill our human destiny.

In the 1970s I got divorced and moved from Switzerland to America, where I was *awakened* as many women were at the time by profound and moving visions of the Divine Feminine. Since then my life has been a day-by-day recognition of all that is lacking in our culture as a result of our not honoring the nurturing aspects of *collective fathering and mothering* in our times—and as a result of this, also not caring for the well-being of the young, the old, the mute, and the vulnerable beings on our planet, including Nature.

I feel like an orphan in a world that is progressively more focused on personal self-sufficiency, because *I know that I cannot serve my deepest values and stockpile for my own survival.* As I stand at this moment on the thin line between the fullness of my strength and its gradual eclipse, I am knowing that once again our generation will need to name and enact whatever it is that will make the aging process one into which we can all (not just the financially self-sufficient) relax with trust, knowing that we have engendered a womb-space for aging, just as through women's sacred circles we created a womb-space for the emergence of Soul, which tended gently and yet powerfully to the emergence of our authentic and empowered younger selves.

My first glimpse of the reality of the aging process in my own life occurred in 1989, when I least expected it. At forty-four years old I felt that I was at the peak of health, creativity, and self-empowerment. I was living at a hot springs retreat center, writing about my *Midwifing the Soul* work with individual women and women in circles, giving workshops on the Soul's growth, practicing massage, and coaching individuals. I knew that I was a fully self-expressed and contributing member of the communities of which I was a part. It was June, and I was about to go to an annual women's summer camp, where for the previous five years I had been a major co-creative member of the staff. Women's camp was always the highlight of my year and the place where I would connect with people and resources that would sustain and excite me for the next year . . . but this year it was not to be. In May, I noticed blood in my stool. I ran to the doctor and underwent a number of invasive tests, the results of which suggested that I might have colon cancer. I was practically ordered to undergo surgery for the removal of a part of my colon within a week of that diagnosis.

Stunned, frightened, and feeling horrible that because of this medical crisis I would not be able to go to the camp, which was to start the next week, I called to let the staff know my situation. The response I received ("*Can't you postpone it? You are letting us down and breaking your contract*") was almost as severe a wake-up call as the diagnosis. *What priorities were being expressed? What really does matter?* When it comes to fulfilling even a spiritually oriented agenda, which is more important, the work, or the person's real-life situation?

This was my first "community teacher," and it opened my mind to the question of what it would mean to be aging in our culture. It was the moment in which I began to seriously envision what would need to happen if I were ever to feel safe in my older, perhaps frail "croning years." I could empathize with the concern that the staff expressed about the hole that would be there if I did not play my part at camp. I would probably have had the same first response if I had been in their shoes. But suddenly everything had changed for me in the light of my potentially terminal illness. I was pulled into a deep recognition of my mortality. Over the ensuing months, I sank deeper and deeper into the questions *What really matters?* and *How do I want to live the rest of my days on this planet?* Since then, my work has never been the same.

Until that time I had lived my life as if I could and would change the world in a big way. When I was thirty-three I was privileged to receive intuitively a vast and compelling vision about the *dawning of the Age of the Daughter.* After that I lived in a world of continuing revelation and inspiration: dancing with this dream, and co-creating with other women a vision for global transformation. My "co-conspirators" and I saw *women making the difference* all over the world. Traveling to distant places, giving big workshops, creating rituals . . . all these things seemed critical to the future healing of our planet. The archetypal world of "the Goddess" was compelling in those early days. Now, overnight, I was suddenly facing possible death from cancer. It was as if a bolt of lightning struck me down in the middle of a serene and sunny day. In an instant, the world shrank down to just me and the question of my bodily survival. The issues that were central to me were now very different. My concern with *saving the world* was temporarily overshadowed by my concern for *saving my own life*. As time went on, the two areas of my concern could no longer be considered apart from each other.

The good news was that it turned out that I did not have cancer . . . just a "pre-cancerous cellular condition"! Nevertheless, my world underwent a radical change. Recovering from surgery took six months. I lost all of my income as a private practitioner. I lost my rented apartment. I lost my ability to take care of myself physically. I became dependent on my younger sister to house me and help me get from place to place, since I could not drive. I used up all of my small savings in covering my daily expenses. And worse than all of that, I found myself feeling *deeply ashamed and guilty* that I had not considered my future needs more carefully, that I was now dependent on my younger sister's resources for survival. In my mind, to be in need of physical and financial help was to be "an object of Christian charity," or a "burden on the State."

I realized that my feelings of shame were mostly due to our cultural conditioning, which teaches us that being self-sufficient is not only noble, but the only way to be. To need what is essentially *mothering and fathering* is not honorable once we leave our teenage years. Culturally, we are expected to undertake and remain on the hero's journey from the moment we leave home until we die—relying only on supernatural interventions from a distant God in times of need. There is a stigma attached to being dependent in one's adult years and

to *needing or asking for help* in any way. Those unfortunate beings in
our culture who cannot pull themselves up by their own bootstraps
are abandoned to their fate. Women who can't make it financially or
intellectually show up in my psyche, and in those of many women I
know, as the fearful spectre of the *homeless bag-lady*. Though I was
residing in a small New Age community at the time I became sick,
even there I did not see care provided for those in need. If you could
work, you could stay. If not, you would have go somewhere else.

The light of my dreams and visions became partially eclipsed as
I struggled to regain my physical and emotional strength. My values
were rearranged. I realized that a summer camp, weekend workshops, profound rituals, and dreams of planetary transformation
were wonderfully idealistic ... but what I wanted now was a "marriage" to a community of women (and men) committed to supporting one another into and through the aging process; a community
that was truthful about all of the real physical and mundane challenges that this stage of life would contain for all of us, sooner or
later. I used to say that the workshop world was "all orgasm and
no marriage." Such wonderful highs and deep intimacy in the
moment ... but then I went home to my local community, where
these values were not part of the culture that surrounded me. It was
as if I had reached the top of a mountain after thinking during the
journey that getting to the top was the final destination. Now I realized that there was in fact another whole piece of life having to do
with *how to live in the valley beyond* with limited resources and failing strength. *Living on the edge* and *living simply* are different; yet I
realized that my value of living simply had *put me on the edge*, and

that unless the larger mainstream community was involved in simple living and intimate connection at the same level that I was, I was
putting myself at risk by continuing to live as if doing the work of my
heart was all that mattered.

With that recognition came a certain level of despair, because
I had always been really sure that we women would be the ones
to make the difference on our planet. *Soul-mothering* had always
been at the heart of my work. Yet here I was, feeling *profoundly
unmothered* by my own spiritual community and *deeply ashamed*
that I needed mothering myself. And as I recovered I realized that I
also needed *fathering* back into life. I needed someone strong and
capable (like the archetypal father) in the outer world to smooth
the way and open new doors for me. *What had gone wrong?* I went to
the depths of my psyche looking for answers and direction, unable
to move forward until I could see a path.

I stopped reading books on spirit and soul, and without consciously thinking about why, I started reading novels about people's
ordinary lives. The life stories of the characters in the novels mirrored
my dilemmas. I felt *met and accompanied* in my confusion and need.
I felt validated in my dawning understanding that real, present, down-
to-earth, committed community is what I needed, and what we all
need, for the human journey beyond "work." Through this reading
undertaken purely intuitively, I came to understand why Angeles
Arrien in her Four-Fold Way work says that "listening to stories that
have meaning to your heart" is healing medicine for issues concerning wounded relationship.

I experience the life of my community, both global and local, to be suffering from *relationship wounding*. Even when my relationships feel deep, the distance between my home and my friends' homes usually prevents us from getting together easily; and if that is not the problem, it is our overcrowded schedules. And I feel overwhelmed by the complexity and the size of the larger community body. I can't connect with it, and I don't understand what it is up to.

The simple fact is that if I am not *present in mind, body, spirit and feelings*; if I am not "in love" and deeply connected in honest relationship with every moment of my life and all that it contains; if I am not *living at the speed of nature* (but instead in the future, in a hoped-for vision), then in my experience I am essentially unsafe, and disconnected from *my* life and *all* life. To be living at the speed of nature is to mother and father myself at the deepest level. To live with others that way is to provide the *nurturing and sustaining presence* for them that true community and family are. For me, to be truly parented is not just to be taken care of, but to be deeply cared for by people who are physically, emotionally, and intellectually close to me . . . and who are available. And I need to be that for others, too.

While before my brush with cancer I had felt profoundly related to the women's spirituality community, I found that after my experience with the hospital I felt like a stranger in a foreign land when I went to women's groups. The topics we explored and celebrated suddenly seemed outdated to me. I was frustrated, lonely, and inarticulate where I had once felt nourished and connected. Clearly I had entered a new chamber of my life-journey, and my companions were not there with me. The Goddess was everywhere, but I could not find the Mother that I feel is essential in a society where children, old people, sick people, and Nature herself need to be tenderly cared for. I asked myself, *Where is the Mother in a community?* She used to be in the family home, but she is hardly home anymore ... and the nuclear family itself seems to be in serious jeopardy these days. So many of us now are not and never have been part of the *procreative family* mode, and family mothers themselves, many of whom are now in the corporations, often have expressed to me their need for mothering and nurturing to alleviate their stress.

During the next five years I found myself in the hospital two more times, and both times were also crisis events. Both times I was told that I might have cancer; both times I underwent major abdominal surgery; and both times it took between four and six months to recover. Each time, my survival resources were consumed, and I returned to my sister's nuclear family home for care and support. Still struggling with a sense of guilt and shame for what I saw as my failure to address reality as it actually is in our society, I finally decided that if I wanted to feel safe and cared for without feeling guilty I had no choice but to *get a job,* a real, in-the-world job with a salary, a pension, sick pay, and disability and unemployment benefits.

Searching for and finding such appropriate employment was a project that brought me to a new level of *disillusionment with the whole notion that security can be found* anywhere *in our societal structure.*

In the course of five years of being employed to do various forms of mothering work for a drug and alcohol abuse prevention agency, the public school system, and a church, I experienced being unable to continue with each of these jobs because, respectively, the pay was

so low that I could not live on it; I was laid off without pay each summer with no guarantee of re-employment in the fall, because funding
was uncertain; and my position was eliminated without notice. I was
working harder and earning less than I ever had as proprietor of my
own counseling and teaching business. I concluded that security, if
there is any, is still as I had always thought it was: in *being real, being
present and responsive to what is, and in doing the work of one's heart.*
The financial support question remained unresolved for me, since it
was clear that for mothering and nurturing work, societal funding was
consistently lacking.

Under these circumstances, hoping to live in a deeply satisfying
mainstream community—in which every member is committed to
the well-being of all the others, and where the purpose of the community is to live and work holistically for the benefit of members,
the earth, and future generations—seemed to be a vague dream
impossible to create. For it would mean swimming against the materialistic corporate business tide, and it is hard to believe that there
are enough of us who care to be able to prevail. So, consciously letting go of concerns for my own security in the future, I re-created
my life and my private practice around the four central values that
make me personally feel safe in each moment as I live it: *Simple,
Deep, Small, and Slow.* It has always gone without saying for me
that my work must also be a *fulfilling* and *authentic* expression of
my Soul's essence, and lead to a day-by-day experience of *balance*
for mind, body, spirit, and feelings. I went back into my own little
world, creating a sense of safety for my clients and myself as best I
could through my work, but I could not forget the question of how

to create a workable community of care for myself in the larger urban setting of Berkeley, where I live.

While I reinvented my life so that it was smaller and more local, slower and more spacious, my closest spiritual sisters seemed to be traveling farther and working in more and more distant places, with larger and larger groups and projects. I felt the distance broadening between their ways of progressing in the transformational work of the Feminine and mine. Over time, I made a point of reducing in size everything I did, and of consciously building beauty and intimacy into all of my work forms. Working mostly in my home, I made my whole space an altar to Sacred Mothering for myself and my clients and friends. I consciously sought clients only from within the boundaries of Berkeley and Oakland. By staying small and going deep with a total community of no more than fifty women, I have felt my work become more deeply fulfilling, and giving me a sense of groundedness that was lacking before. Yet the question of community for myself still hangs uneasily around the edges of my mind, as over and over again my friends and I search our calendars often four or five weeks in advance of the present day for a time when we will be free to meet!

What is it that I want as I continue to age? This has become the central question of my life, and one that overwhelms me as I try to think it through.

In my ponderings one day, I remembered that early in 1999 I had been introduced to the work of economist Marilyn Waring, a brilliant, powerful, heart-centered New Zealand woman who became a member of that country's Parliament at the age of twenty-one and subsequently made a video (called "Who's Counting") on the topic of how the corporate economy works, and what kinds of work are even counted as economically valuable. She demonstrated through cross-cultural research that the work of *nourishing, caring for, and sustaining life*—which is generally taken on by women—is rarely counted as being of any economic value whatsoever. And when it *is* counted, it is usually compensated at minimum wage, or close to it. She demonstrated scientifically that *mothering is almost universally of "no economic value" to the profit-driven mainstream cultures in which we live.* Those who mother physically, emotionally, or spiritually must come to terms with living at a subsistence level, or working till they drop—holding down their mothering tasks as well as a job that pays well so that they can cover their bills.

Unless one is either a member of a close-knit and generous nuclear family (which is rare these days), or the inheritor of substantial wealth or a guaranteed means of livelihood (also relatively rare); or unless one joins the corporate conspiracy and succumbs to its stressful requirements for success (much more common!), one cannot expect to sustain oneself safely in old age.

Of this I became painfully aware at a level that I had never felt it before in the early months of this year. The "Y2K" challenge made it clear to me. And at that time I became aware that along with me, the whole world might be in a dilemma of "social insecurity" if, as predicted by so many cutting-edge thinkers, *the world as we know it* fell apart. Luckily for us it did not happen this time, but ecological realities inform us that if we do not make a clear turn in at least one if not many different directions very soon, *the world as we know it* will be a vanishing phenomenon before this millennium is much older.

It is clear to me that it is as true now as it has been throughout history—*to have real "social security" is to have a sense of family and village or tribe to which one can turn at any time, and on a regular basis, for nonmonetary resources.* The question is, how can those of us who do not have a nuclear family in the places where we live (or anywhere at all) create something like it? Every year there seem to be more of us in this position, and with this need.

In March 1999 I began to write down a vision for a *holistic, skillful, nurturing, and sustainable community*—the kind of community that could form itself in any urban neighborhood, and that I could gladly commit to for the rest of my life. It would be constellated through existing women's circles, but it would also include men and children. I wrote without stopping for more than a month, giving words to this new part of the vision for healing on our planet that has always been embedded in my Soul—one that will still take a huge amount of energy and commitment on the part of caring and inspired women and men who really want to be part of *inciting the world to caring evolution*. I believe it to be workable.

I see the formation of neighborhood collectives of seven small circles with a maximum of eight people in each one, circles that will come together intentionally as a committed *community tribe* whose intention it is to facilitate what Joanna Macy calls "The Great Turning." My vision, entitled "Communities for the Great Turning," calls for a maximum number of fifty-six individuals (women, men, and children) who come together intentionally to create a different way of being within the larger urban communities in which they live. Such communities will divide and multiply as they reach maximum desirable membership size, and they will intentionally become skillful in clearly defined ways. The number of groups in the collective is suggested to me by the *seven fundamental areas of human need* that are named in every spiritual tradition; i.e., 1. *Physical survival*, 2. *Emotional nurturing*, 3. *Personal fulfillment*, 4. *Compassionate service to community*, 5. *Creative expression*, 6. *Intuition, and 7. Communion with Universal Spirit.*

I suggest eight as the maximum number of members in each circle, because it allows for one masculine and one feminine representative for each direction on the wheel of life: each season of the year. The number fifty-six is also about the size of three generations of an extended nuclear family, and as such it represents to me *the largest number of individuals for whom I can really care—physically, emotionally, and spiritually*—over time, and in an ongoing and grounded way.

It's a big dream, and it will take a while to take root and bloom. Outreach may be slow, but I do believe that within half an hour's walking distance or ten minutes' drive from my house there are fifty-six people to whom I can relate intellectually, physically, and emotionally, and who could and would commit to such a process of self-transformation, community visioning, and healing.

Now, in these first few tender days of the year 2000, having witnessed the community celebrations of both midnight and dawn in so many countries of the world over the satellite TV connections that united people everywhere for those precious moments in time . . . it is as if I were playing a flute on a hill in the darkest night of winter. Even though I am not sure that anyone is out there tuning in to the realm of *mysterious and invisible connection* that I am tapping into . . . some people may recognize the distant tones of a tune that drifts in through an open window in their consciousness, and know that they have been writing other parts of this *Symphony for a Subtle Evolution*.

Whether this is so or not, I am personally going ahead by *deepening my commitment to the sanity of each moment and to the value of relationship everywhere in my life*. I am putting my focus on locating and committing to a *tribe of choice*, and I am imagining myself recognizing them one by one, and welcoming them into my life . . . all fifty-six of them. We will eat, sing, dance, laugh, and celebrate the turning of seasons together . . . and the next time my body, or theirs, gives out, we will know who our family is, and that we will be there for each other.

Call me if you live within ten minutes' driving or half an hour's walking distance of Arch Street in North Berkeley, California. Perhaps we are part of the same tribe?

MARIA GABRIELLE

Maria Gabrielle, N.D., was born in Reading, Pennsylvania, and spent most of her life on the East Coast teaching biology and overseeing various entrepreneurial ventures. While visiting New Mexico, she was captivated by the natural beauty and spiritual energy of Santa Fe and moved there with her husband, Cliff Kroski. During her doctoral studies in Naturopathy, she studied in both the United States and Europe, specializing in biological medicine. In 1992, she founded Alternative Therapy Associates, a holistic health center where patients come from all over the country for treatment. Dr. Gabrielle is currently Director of Alternative Therapy Associates, a professor at the University of Natural Medicine and Executive Director of Kinship Institute, a dream which is in the process of becoming a reality. She also teaches seminars to health professionals on biological medicine topics. She lives in Santa Fe with her wonderful husband and two beautiful dogs, Antara and Shadow.

Keep Going, Keep Growing

My mother started her own catering business on a shoestring when she turned sixty-one, and very successfully kept it going for twelve years. That took courage. But if you'd ask her, she'd tell you that it was a logical next step. My mom has never stopped moving forward. She's full of surprises. What an example she has been for me!

From a very young age, my parents convinced me that I could do anything or become anyone I wanted to be, as long as I was willing to work hard and take responsibility. I've never doubted that. It is one of the deep beliefs that have supported me throughout the years. Looking back over my life, I realize that it has been a collage of experience and learning—each piece fitting into the other, each having its own uniqueness, each falling into the general theme, "Keep going, keep growing."

As I sit here writing this piece, I begin to wonder about this experience called life. The age-old questions come to mind—What is it really all about? Why are we here? What is the purpose of it all?

Just as my brain finishes asking these questions, my eyes serendip-itously fall upon a small slip of paper on which, weeks ago, I copied a bit of wisdom from Pir ViLayat Inayat Khan. He says, "The purpose of life is that God should attain through you a further advance in the evolution of the universe."

I begin to question, "Has that happened through my life?" I find myself answering, timidly, "I hope so." Then I get real, and say resoundingly, "Yes, I really think it has!"

As far back as I can remember, I have used my heart and gut, with a little mind thrown in now and then, to make all the major decisions that have given shape to this lifetime. Some of them seemed to make no logical or financial sense—yet they all worked out in the end, and became the stepping-stones to the next adventure.

Taking risks has never been a problem. When I go with my gut feel-ing, it doesn't really feel like a risk, though it might objectively appear as such. There is a sense of "knowing" with which we women are gifted. We can choose to take advantage of it or not. And that sense of "know-ing" can guide the lives of those who attune to it. It was tuning in to that sense of knowing, and making use of that intuitive spark, that I believe has allowed my life to flow from one career to the next. Now I can see how each individual piece was necessary for what is now developing.

After college, I became a biology teacher. I taught for ten years, but then felt myself "burning out" and didn't think I'd be effective as a teacher any longer. I next took a job with a church, doing social work with the poor and elderly, and filling various administrative and cre-ative functions within the parish community. After five years of finan-cial struggle, I began part-time work in the real-estate industry to supplement my income. This eventually became a full-time job, which often had me working days, evenings, and weekends. The stress and lack of rest brought on a serious illness.

It was during this time that I married a wonderful man who has been a loving support over the past fifteen years. Cliff and I and two beautiful dogs make up our family.

The illness was a rare muscle disease which ended up being the catalyst to my medical career. Traditional allopathic medicine held no answers for me. The doctors said, "No cure, just steroids to relieve the pain." After giving that route a short try, I said, "Thanks, but no thanks," and set out on a journey of self-healing so intriguing that it changed my life forever.

I view that illness as a divine gift. As a result of it, my life changed and suddenly went in two directions simultaneously. I began to study natural medicine to find ways of healing myself—not realizing at the time that eventually I would become a naturopathic doctor, and use the knowledge I had gained to help many others. At the same time, I opened a small maternity consignment shop, which within a year grew into a larger retail business. This was used as a source of income to support my studies in alternative medicine.

Three years later, with the consignment shop still in operation, "Inner Light" was established. This was a center for various holistic modalities as well as an esoteric and holistic bookstore. It was with a tremendous amount of joy that I opened this center, because by this time, alternative medicine had become a passion.

A few years later, I happened to go to Santa Fe, New Mexico, to do some spiritual work. What can I say? I fell in love with its overwhelming beauty and felt totally at home immediately. It is very appropriately called the Land of Enchantment. With my husband's openness and willingness to take risks, we moved to the Southwest soon thereafter. I went on to get my doctorate in naturopathy, and I have been practicing ever since.

I need to mention that a very important thread that has been woven throughout every part of my life is the spiritual thread. In my younger days, it was a spirituality wrapped within the framework of religion. It evolved into a spirituality that comes from deep within — an unshakable belief that "All things do indeed work unto good. . . ."

These days I am involved in a project called Kinship Institute. Let me share with you how this new piece of my life's collage came about.

Not too long ago someone asked me, "If money were no object, what would you do next? What would be the dream you'd follow?" It didn't take me long to reply that I'd like to create a project that would help make the world a kinder, gentler, healthier place to live. From the response to that question, the vision of Kinship Institute was given birth — a vision that is currently in the process of becoming a reality — a vision that embodies much that I hold dear and sacred.

I am fortunate to be working with a group of uniquely gifted and inspiring professionals in creating a center which will be about holistic education in every sense of the words. We intend both to teach and to be a living model of what we teach.

Housed in totally nontoxic buildings, surrounded by nature's beauty, Kinship Institute will be a teaching center for classes in physical, emotional/psychological, and spiritual wholeness. It will include a greenhouse, an organic garden, a bookstore, and an animal facility, complete with a holistic veterinarian—together with our current alternative medical office. There will also be outdoor and indoor areas for quiet reflection and meditation. Along with the teaching, we intend to do scientific research around the effectiveness of spiritual healing, using hands-on and energy processes, and alternative methods of creating health.

The main purpose of Kinship Institute is to promote awareness of the beauty, sacredness, and kinship of all life, and to foster ways of living that are in alignment with that understanding. We maintain that personal well-being is inextricably linked to healthy relationships with animals, plants, and the earth itself.

An ambitious project? You bet! Lots of work? Absolutely! But a labor of love.

Being executive director of Kinship Institute requires, along with an entrepreneurial spirit, experience in natural medicine, education, real estate, business administration, and public relations—all nestled within a solid spiritual base.

Following my intuition and recognizing and nurturing my God/Goddess-given gifts have brought me to this wonderful moment in time. I look back on all the facets of my life and my heart sings. Through all the hardship and struggle, through all the moments of joy, laughter, and quiet prayer, a sacred thread was being woven, my destiny was being created. I often did not fully understand why I was drawn toward doing something or meeting someone, but I always trusted that feeling inside that said, "Do it!" I see now that my entire life has been a preparation for this work.

So why have I taken you on this journey through my life? To illustrate a truth that I'm sure I have lived in common with many of you who are reading this—that if we are open and willing, all of our life's experiences will lead us to just where we need to be.

ANN O'NEAL GARCIA

In sixty years of living, here's what Ann O'Neal Garcia has to crow about: a surprisingly long marriage of thirty-nine years to Tony; their two kids—Johnathan, who at thirty-eight is back in college and making A's on his English papers, and Carolyn, who just published her first book, a read-aloud called Moonboy *(Moonboy himself is her only grandchild to date); her twenty-four years in the trenches of public school teaching in Cheyenne, Wyoming; the publication of her book,* Spirit on the Wall; *her present job as Writing Center tutor at Highlands University in Las Vegas, New Mexico; her wonderful, wonderful friends who keep her sane and happy; and her deep and abiding love for nature and for God.*

"There's Life in the Old Dame Yet..."

With my grandmothers and mother long gone, who can teach me graceful acceptance of aging? Who can show me what really matters when I look in the mirror and see my face acquiring surprising new wrinkles? For answers and inspiration, I turn to my friends in our writers' group, fourteen vital women, who know how life after fifty is to be lived.

My writers' group is more to me than a bunch of sharp critiquers. They've become family, and these powerful ladies are my role models. It's not only what they say, even though they are wise and funny; it's their zest for life, sharp and sweet as hand-squeezed lemonade, that I drink for wisdom. Seated next to my friends, hunched over the manuscript we'll be dealing with this evening, I consider what Mehitabel the cat joyously told her friend: "There's life in the old dame yet." I'll drink to that. *Another round!* I think, as I look from one animated face to the other.

Every other Sunday we meet at Marva's house, where the silent-screen cowboy, Tom Mix, used to live. It's a livelier mix than it ever

was, as our raucous laughter and enthusiastic voices bounce off the
faded pink wallpaper and practically quiver the tall, skinny window-
panes. We critique—well and thoroughly, and with love—each
manuscript, like helping birth a baby, and we take our midwifing seriously. We've had two weeks to write commentaries in the margins of
the manuscripts we'll review tonight. No gentle "tea party," the group
can be painfully honest. When we need to, we will say, "That just
doesn't work for me," but we're quick to scribble big stars next to anything that does. Here are stars for a well-turned phrase, a powerful
verb, realistic dialogue.

A diverse group, we have a few outward signs of commonality.
We're all female and we are not young anymore, ranging in age from
fifty-something to eighty. We wear comfy clothes—we've sworn off
tight girdles, high heels, constricting hosiery, and shoes that pinch.
Some of our differences are obvious. We come in shades of colors:
black, brown, and a Heinz variety of white. Other differences aren't
immediately obvious. Our belief systems run a wide gamut from
Roman Catholic to metaphysical to agnostic. We've lived all over
the planet: Ireland, Estonia, the Far East, America from coast to
coast; a few have stayed here in Las Vegas, New Mexico, all their
lives. Three women are college professors; a few didn't get any farther than high school. We represent the married, widowed, single,
significant-othered, divorced; some have children, grandchildren,
even great-grandchildren. We write historical fiction, science fiction,
poetry, young-adult books, essays, mainstream genre fiction, and
some works that defy classification. We celebrate our differences as
we bring our life experiences to the table. Someone knows the types

of flowers that grow along the southern coast of England. The little lady who still speaks in Bronx-Jewish accent can tell you the exact make and model of a gun perfect for your mystery. The woman serving coffee returned to college after getting her family raised. She can tick off a list of the poisons used in the time of Louis XIV, in case you ever need to know.

Marva, tiny and twinkly as an elf, tries to bring the meeting to order. She speaks so softly that she has to clang silverware on a glass to get attention. "We have work to do!" Pushing eighty, Marva has just written her first illustrated children's novel, an enchanting tale of mice interacting with human beings. In her spare time, she tutors kids who need help learning to read and write. Charmingly fey, she coaxes reluctant readers into a change of heart and intellect before they know what hit them. And she never charges a penny for her services.

As we get into the round-table critiquing, Betsy and Brent, who are sisters, begin using sign language. Are they saying, "Oh, brother! Alberta's going on too long again"? They learned signing late in life, so they could communicate with a dear friend who is almost deaf.

Betsy, a world-class proofreader who never misses a dangling participle, squints at the manuscript and pens in a few words. Sometimes she works as an extra in films made around here. "The movie industry seems to love funny-looking little old ladies," she's told us. In her sixties, Betsy is a veteran with nine movies under her belt, and she's been a featured extra twice. Recently she worked in *All the Pretty Horses*, decked out as a waitress from the forties. One day, director Billy Bob Thornton came over to her as she sat in the make-up trailer. "You look so familiar," he told her. "Like a member of my family."

Brent signs something else to her sister. A published writer, Brent is always fine-tuning her epic, a trilogy about the Southwest Indians who were conquered during Coronado's time. She knows her anthropology, and her words take us into another time, into the complex and beautiful culture the Indians enjoyed before the vast armies from Spain forever changed their lives.

A master of rewrite, Brent has revised the book so many times even she has lost count. But she takes time out every summer for her grandkids, who sometimes stay with her nearly three months. Her house is then transformed; the kids' wild chalk drawings on the sidewalk point the way to her front door, and there's some scribbling near her picture window which won't rub out. This summer, a granddaughter created incredible art on Brent's new computer. "She used up all my ink," Brent grouses, sneaking out a sample of Jessica's creations during a pause in the meeting. Perpetually young at heart, Brent's attitude about aging is, "Forget it! People are younger today, partly because they're healthier and partly because nobody tells them they have to be old."

Every Christmas Eve, Brent and her husband host a huge party. The guest list is organic, always growing, even though their house isn't. Each year they manage to squeeze in at least one more, particularly if a newcomer to the writers' group might otherwise have a lonesome holiday. We arrive for the party wildly costumed and hyped for our individual vaudeville acts, which follow the potluck meal. We wonder excitedly: will Lil, who's seventy-eight but never acts it, play the nose-harp again?

Beginning her critique, Lil puts on her glasses, which dangle from a string around her neck. When she writes and shares, we're in stitches over her comical essays. Often they're about growing up as an only child on the grounds of an institution for the mentally retarded, where her dad was head psychiatrist. Surprisingly down-to-earth, Lil also sews cloth sculptures for the young kids in her life and for art shows. My favorite is her rounded, sexy Venus of Willendorf, fashioned from soft, faded fabrics.

It's Jane's turn to speak, and she raises her orange eyebrows and says, "I hardly know where to begin." The author leans forward and seems to hold her breath. Does this beginning comment portend a positive review—or otherwise? With Jane, you don't second-guess, but you can be sure of one thing: she'll not spare the truth. And she knows what she's talking about. Not only does she churn out a couple of novels every year, she paints dozens of pictures and still manages to teach English at a local college. She's generous, too—giving us tips about agents who might be interested in our stuff, reporting on writers' conferences she's attended, and lending out her library of literary magazines. "There's not enough literature about older women," she often proclaims. Like a hound after a faint scent, she searches for that market and lets us know when she's found a lead.

Johanna is new to the group. To keep herself fed, she's an accountant, and at tax time, we rush to her for help: but her passion is for her art. She shapes haunting ceramic sculptures, mostly women's faces— some serene, some very troubled—and when we view them, we see ourselves, the many sides of our psyches. If these glimpses make us uncomfortable, so does the subject matter of her writing.

Originally from Estonia, Johanna has just finished translating the diaries her mother wrote during World War II. After losing her father in the war, Johanna and her family were deported to the United States in 1950 and dropped into a strange new world in North Dakota. They didn't speak the language and they were flat broke. Her mother, a highly educated woman and a trained artist, went to work immediately as a washerwoman in an old people's home. I take lessons from Johanna's mother. When I bathe, I'm grateful I'm not squatting under a cold-water tap in a refugee camp. When I sit down in my living room, I thank God for this peaceful place, where bombs aren't screaming into the nearby streets. Johanna's mother, Helene, has joined our group, too, her voice as real as anyone's sitting here at the table, even though she died many years ago.

Sarah is one in our group who has gone through the most dramatic recent changes. After a family life with a husband and six kids, she found herself lonely when her husband died and the baby of the family grew up and moved away. Through counseling and reading, she realized she might be gay. Great with follow-through, it wasn't long before she found the perfect woman partner. When she fell in love, she was transformed into a person whose feet didn't quite touch the ground. This flightiness seemed paradoxical in a woman who taught us folk dancing and encouraged us to stomp our feet to the rhythms of other countries. After she and her partner moved in together, they soon formed yet another group, this for people wanting to become fluent in Spanish. At seventy, Sarah exemplifies the spark that can occur when changes in lifestyle are in order.

Some of the women in our writing group live out of town, and drive many miles over rut-filled roads to join us at Marva's. Rebecca, leaning way back in her chair, has driven her old rattly truck twenty-six miles to get here. She lives in the country, makes her own bread and cheese, harvests a rich variety of tomatoes, peppers, eggplants, and cucumbers—and since her place doesn't have running water, she's rigged up a system of tanks and pipes that do the job. She lives alone, likes it that way, and regularly contributes articles to a local newspaper.

After three hours of intensive work, we're wrapping up the meeting. Tonight we've critiqued two chapters of a murder mystery, a short story, and three literate, lyrical poems. We file out of Marva's old house charged with a renewed love and respect for one another and for the literature we're making.

The night is crisp and clean; there's sheet lightning shuddering behind the clouds and outlining their edges in silver. I think about an impending deadline for an article, upset that it's due before I can run it by the group.

I watch Rebecca climb into her truck. She grins widely from her weather-beaten face, then guns the engine trying to get it going good before she lets out the clutch. I watch her vehicle lurch away from the curb, follow it as the taillights wink when she stops at the corner. She's going home, all alone, to dark acreage. I guess I can manage the article by myself. It's one of the lessons my group of women is teaching me. I square my shoulders and bid my friends—my sisters, my mothers, my grandmothers—goodbye till next time.

EDNA C. GROVES

For twenty-five years, Edna C. Groves of Naperville, Illinois, has taught women's workshops which have evolved along with her own questing and learning. In this way she personally and professionally explored such themes as the mother/daughter relationship, women and our relationship to food, learning to love the body you have, honoring anger, developing self-esteem, journal-writing, developing resilience, creating personal boundaries, and taking risks. She loves to be with women who are asking questions and expanding. One of her current themes comes of being in her mid-sixties: Celebrating the Seasoned Woman. Another is the exploration of women's risk-taking, with appreciation for the mythic heroism lived by ordinary women leading everyday lives.

Finding home

I'm thinking about home at almost the end of my trip, and I don't want to go home. I want to continue on the road. I'm surprised and dismayed by this. I've been gone almost six weeks. It's time in a few days to leave this week-long writing workshop in Duluth and point the nose of my small Roadtrek van toward the suburb of Chicago where I live. A comfortable day's drive, it'll be the last leg of a 5,800-mile, five-week journey. Along the way, I've enjoyed a textured mix of contact with family and friends; I've sampled rich solitude, adventure, and roaming in beautiful places; and I've capped the long and stimulating trip by immersion in this exciting travel-writing program. I've never had this kind of adventure before. I want more. I don't want to go home.

Home. Such a loaded word, carrying images similar across cultures—the actual hearth of fire, and the metaphorical hearth of warmth, welcome, food, comfort—a haven in a weary world. "It is the place of renewal and of safety, where for a little while there will be no harm or attack and, while every sense is nourished, the soul rests," writes May Sarton. Without question, it's a place we crave and count on.

We each carry unique and personal memories of homes from our past. These homes are real inside us, even when we no longer live in them, or when the houses no longer exist. I remember the layout of the house of my childhood in Brooklyn, the well-used furniture in each room, even the placement of windows and closets. I can see the familiar kitchen—where the old white stove was, and who stood over it; the table, and who sat where; the odd tomato color of the painted walls; the everyday dishes and their floral markings; the ornate scrolling on the silverware; certain worn, yet shiny pots and pans, and special serving dishes; a breadbox in the corner of the sideboard; a set of salt and pepper shakers, tops slightly dusted with their contents.

Aromas float back from memory—fragrances of my favorite foods, what the house smelled like when I came in from play. I remember family rituals for celebratory times. I hold visions of neighbors and the neighborhood—where the good trees were for climbing and hide-and-seek; the cracks in the sidewalk; street games, stores we ran errands to, places where we ate ice cream in the hot summer. The kids I played with; the kids I didn't.

We grow up and leave our childhood homes and eventually create homes of our own, perhaps with other people. Every day we see the place we currently inhabit, with landscaping we have inherited or chosen, furnished with objects of our choice, and peopled with our loves, two- and four-legged. Perhaps our current homes contain ghosts of people who were once here with us, or people who were never here in body but whom we carry inside. We live here now, love here, do our work-in-the-world from here; we cook and eat and play here, welcome friends. We return to this home gratefully from our forays into "the real world." We nourish ourselves here.

I like my current home. I've lived in it with my husband for thirteen years. I like my quiet tree-shaded neighborhood, too. For over thirty years, I've been living in this same Chicago suburb, where we raised our four daughters. I've practiced psychotherapy, taught, and led workshops here for twenty-two years, and I am embedded in a strong network of longtime friends, professional contacts, and spiritual affiliation. I am well-rooted. Yet I don't want to go home.

I began this journey over five weeks ago, with my beloved black lab Buddy as companion and protector. I drove to eastern Minnesota to join my friends Harriet and Sarah and their Roadtrek. They offered to travel tandem with me at the beginning of my trip, teaching me tricks of the road they'd learned on earlier trips. In our vans, sharing friendship, talk, laughter, food, and driving, we caravanned to Butte, Montana, where we went our separate ways. Feeling strong and self-reliant, I tooled along through Idaho, then Oregon, where two of my daughters and their families reside, and then on to Washington State, where my friends and I again linked up for a few days in Fort Casey State Park on Whidbey Island. When we parted on Whidbey, I soloed for two glorious weeks, traveling along U.S. 2 across the northern edge of the United States until I arrived in Duluth for the writing workshop. I was on my own, free and full of joy in my adventure.

The seed for this solo journey had been planted on Whidbey Island three years earlier. After two years of soul-searching, I had just closed my psychotherapy practice and let go of the office I'd had for

fifteen professionally important years. After a long and deeply satisfying relationship and a prolonged and difficult ending, psychotherapy and I were finally finished with each other. I believed that if I
paused in my life I would discover within that space the next unfolding step of my life purpose. Earlier life experience helped me to
learn of the power of the void. I would wait, alert to new possibilities
that would reveal to me clues about my next direction. In some discomfort, I tried to curb my impatience and just live with not knowing what was next. I knew I had more to contribute—in my early
sixties, I was seasoned and had much to offer—but I just didn't yet
see the way to do it.

I was on Whidbey with fourteen other women and one man who
had collaborated several times over two years with Christina Baldwin
and Ann Linnea, cofounders of PeerSpirit, an organization dedicated
to bringing the circle form back into our western culture. We were all
actively interested in this form. Janel, closest to me in age of all the
participants, had taken some of her recent divorce settlement and,
rather than settle into a condo, had bought a Roadtrek, a very small
motor home in which she intended to be a perpetual nomad. I was
intrigued by her Roadtrek. I remember seeing the interior of it, and
my immediate excitement and the clear thought, "I could do this.
I could travel this way."

For weeks after the collaborative ended, thoughts and images of
Janel and her van remained constant. After several weeks, the image
grew to contain the addition of a good-sized dog, a picture which further refined itself into a male black labrador. I knew that I had to
hold the images, keep silent, and wait to see if they faded or held firm.

They held for months. I'd had this experience before. I knew that outside of my conscious, planning, purposeful mind, another process was beginning to unfold from underneath, in a way with which I had finally become familiar, if not always initially comfortable. I knew once again that I was being beckoned into a self-expansion that I might not understand, yet would be strongly drawn to. The words of the fourteenth-century Catholic mystic Meister Eckhart, important to me at earlier times of my life, came up again, and stayed:

> *When the soul wishes to have an experience of herself*
> *she creates an image of that experience*
> *and then steps into it.*

When I knew the dream was not going to go away, I began to discuss it with my husband. No stranger to my needs for personal expansion, he wrestled with what my dream meant to him. The acquisition of a dog in our relatively free existence gave him more trouble than the possibility of a small motorhome. But over the next year he gradually shifted to accept the idea of having a dog. Three days after he agreed to it, Buddy showed up through Labrador Rescue. Three months after that, in March 1999, a gently used Roadtrek turned up. We bought it, and I began to plan my adventure.

As I began to share my trip plans with others, I noticed startlingly different responses from men than from women. In general, the men responded with envy or wistfulness, saying, "I wish I could be doing that," "You're lucky," "As soon as I retire I'm going to head out myself." In general, the women's responses were fear-based, either about their own fears, as in, "I'd be too afraid to make such a trip alone," "No way could I do that," "You're going by *yourself*?" or with assumptions about my lack of fear—either that I had none: "You must not be afraid," or flat-out, "You are really brave," or wondering, "Aren't you scared?"

I was afraid before the trip, and I was uneasy at moments during the trip. I believe that courage admits the presence of fear, which is, after all, a signal to take care of ourselves so that we can continue to move toward living our dreams. I grew up in Brooklyn, New York, with some experience of prowlers, home invaders, and flashers. I remember several years ago buying a novel, *Places in the World a Woman Could Walk*, purely on my reaction to the title. Where were these places of safety? I had to work to help my dreams transcend my fears, and to deal with the balancing of risk, caution, and freedom.

One of the continuing tensions I experienced while traveling alone was the pull between my desire to move alone and freely through the natural world, and the constant awareness that, if I did, I might not be safe. Yet my concerns before the trip were not focused on my personal safety as much as on the what-ifs of vehicle malfunction or accident. When I wanted to scare myself, I imagined my van coming to a halt on a remote two-lane highway with no help in sight. How would I manage? Would I know what to do? Who would help me? Whom could I trust?

I suspected that some of my deeper and more frightening concerns about personal safety as a woman traveling alone were displaced onto something I could stand to focus on and plan ahead for—vehicle breakdown. My husband helped me learn about the workings of the van. A careful reading of the vehicle's warranty showed I was covered for roadside assistance. I also had my cell phone, and Buddy, whose protectiveness toward me had become obvious. No one would know that his deep-throated bark and generous size masked a marshmallow. Eventually I decided my safeguards were enough. Once I realized that, I began to notice an important inner shift: I too was enough. I had resources. I could more than cope with what turned up. I just wouldn't deliberately put myself at physical risk. On a bright, clear, sunny Monday morning in mid-June, two and a half years from the beginning of my dream, I left home, exhilarated and finally on my way.

I've had lots of solitude in my life—and never enough—and yet I was surprised at the joy I experienced in the two weeks of solitary travel. I was amazed by the fleeting yet steady upcroppings of joy as I skimmed along the northern edge of the country, marveling at the beauty of the land surrounding the ribbon of U.S. 2. I smelled freedom, I felt freedom's winds caressing my skin, I danced with freedom and clothed myself in it. I kept looking for places where I could let Buddy run free; eventually I caught on that Buddy's freedom was mine too. A journal note: "Maybe I'm becoming an ecstatic." Tearful, I felt grateful for the people I love, for those who love me, for my health, for enough time, money, and support to help this dream of a journey become real.

To risk, I knew, means leaving safe, familiar, predictable relationships or surroundings in order to try out unknown, unpredictable, and promising new parts of ourselves. I know my need to risk came from a deep need to stretch beyond my previous ways of being, to enact longings for adventure, "to dwell," as Anais Nin wrote, "in possibility." In order to live this dream, I had to move through my fears. What I got back were profound experiences of joy and freedom beyond anything I'd ever known, and a deeply liberating sense of being at home in myself. I don't have to be on the road to be home. I don't have to go home to be home. Wherever I am, I am home in me.

MARGARET JAMISON

Margaret Jamison started her adult life earlier than most, and lived her life in reversed form. A spouse, children, a house—all hers to manage until there was space to begin the university student life. She earned her undergraduate degree in twelve years, her master's in four, and her doctorate in two, after which she gave herself a graduation party at the age of forty-five. As she has grown older, she has found women seeking her out because of the way she lived her life and pursued her dreams. So, almost without realizing it or intending it, she has become a mentor. In turn, her work as a psychotherapist brings her close to the interior spaces of her clients, and as she listens, she becomes more clear about her own changing interior as well. Outside her consulting room, she is a writer of fiction and poetry because . . . she must.

The Crones are In!

I am a crone. I grew into the idea slowly, and with resistance. Since I was told early in life that I took after my grandmother and would some day resemble her, I developed a keen interest in old women and what they looked like. Hiding behind my attractive mother while she shopped, I stared at the old women. Frail, spindly-legged women teetered precariously in the store aisles, and were often eclipsed by a sisterhood of tubby women, puffing as they waddled along. I shuddered and promised myself I would not become one of "them." I wondered what my mother's fate would be.

I struggled with my dread of being a woman and growing old. When I reached my thirties, I did not look like my childhood image of old. I didn't have a hooked nose, nor blue hair. Instead, I had a stark awareness of how few women held positions of power. In search of role models, I started reading biographies of famous women. My distress increased. Their lives didn't resemble mine in the slightest. I continued to struggle with my dread of being a woman who would someday be old.

My entrance into the fourth decade was marked by an explosion of books about the mysterious and innate woman power. Change echoed on a personal level as well. In the middle of the decade, I completed my Ph.D. in psychology and opened a private practice as a psychotherapist. The women's spirituality movement blossomed, sending out new shoots into tradition-bound domains. Women I knew were asking questions and redefining themselves. Herstory, not his, began to take form. I read of the matriarchy, and the treatment of women by the male-dominated power structure. Alice Walker wrote *The Color Purple*. *The Female Eunuch* sat on my bedside table. Copies of *Ms. Magazine* cluttered the floor. A shift took place. When I celebrated my forty-ninth birthday, I had glimmers of a direction I wanted to pursue. I would stand in line for entry into the world of wise, powerful, knowing old women. I found an ambivalent comfort when I realized I was not alone in my dilemma about facing old age as a woman.

I discovered Barbara G. Walker's *The Crone*. She urges her readers to seek understanding of the "wise, willful, wolfish Crone." Her writing captivated my spirit. Probability became tangible.

However, I could take my time about becoming a crone. I continued to bask in my relative youthfulness. I told myself I wasn't quite there yet.

A friend in her sixties told me of Judith Duerk's superb book, *I Sit Listening to the Wind*, which validates women's roles as transmitters of knowledge and keepers of wisdom. Her images of legions of girls and young women negotiating major passages of their lives without much guidance or instruction resonated deep in my being. Duerk poses the

question, "How would your life have been different if you could have
sat in a circle of older women who could help you, who would listen
to your anguish and confusion, and share their knowledge with you?"
I wept at the idea of how my life might have been, had there been a
circle of crones with whom I could have consulted at those critical
transition points. What would the course of my life have been had I
sat surrounded by wise women when I discovered at age sixteen that
I had become pregnant from a rape by an ex-boyfriend? I didn't tell
anyone about the rape. I didn't even know the word! Instead I carried
my shame and the fetus simultaneously. How might my life have been
different when I blamed myself for the death of a childhood friend?
Could a circle of crones have helped me come to terms with my grief
and guilt? What would my choices have been, at other critical points
in my years as a younger woman and mother, if I could have been surrounded by crones to counsel and guide me?

I knew that many women of all ages were isolated and afraid as
they faced turning points in their lives. Fifty-five years had made some
marks on more than just my skin. I heard many, many stories. There
were no wisdom-dispensing crones standing outside supermarkets.
Women were changing their minds about many things, mostly in
internal, private ways. I let the issue of how to behave as a crone sink
in and percolate in some quiet recess in my mind, knowing from
experience to let the material marinate in its own juices and cook.
Transformation and creation would bubble up from the pot when
they were ready for tasting.

Around that time, I had the good fortune to be invited to join a
consulting group with other psychotherapists, men and women.

Eventually, the group, without direction or determination, became a group of only women. We were a quartet, women in our fifties and sixties. After some months of meeting regularly, we realized how much help we were receiving from one another, not only with challenging cases we would bring for group consultation, but with thorny, troublesome, and often tough situations in our personal lives. One morning I confessed to a formidable situation surrounding one of my adult sons. My colleagues suddenly transformed themselves into that circle of wise older women that Duerk had described, and for which I had longed. The incubation period from Duerk's book ended. Here in front of my eyes was the answer. As a group of four, we had something strong and powerful to offer other women. We were all crones!

What happened next was as exciting and thrilling as any endeavor I have ever undertaken, either professionally or personally. After I soaked up the goodness and wise counsel from my colleagues, I made reference to the Duerk book, describing its thesis briefly. I added that in their presence I had encountered what Duerk had described. As if speaking with a single voice, the four of us immediately identified an unexpressed wish. We wanted to find a way to share with other women the richness we gave to one another during our meeting times. As seasoned meeting-goers, we knew that our meetings were exceptional, and what all meetings strive to be. Our meetings were smooth, rich, egalitarian, and flowing. When an outcome occurred, it was balanced and we felt blessed.

Over the next two sessions, we sketched out a plan to implement our common dream. We decided to begin a series that we titled "The Crones Are In!" The next idea flowed as effortlessly as a snow-fed stream in spring. We would do our crone circles on the vernal and autumnal equinoxes and winter and summer solstices. We were in completely new, unexplored territory with each other as we put forth our ideas. We knew each other's professional stances well, and acknowledged our diverse training as mental health professionals. We respected the differences in our approaches to psychotherapy. We didn't know as much about where we were in relation to one another about our personal values, beliefs, philosophies, and hopes. What we discovered was an elegant, harmonious but distinct vision we each carried.

Our shared dream was to help other women confront life's issues without disabling fear, to help them move instead with self-compassion and identification into a new way of moving in the world. We would be role models to those who were troubled by growing old and being women. We could join those women, as crows in an ancient forest . . . together.

When I announced to friends that I had joined with three other psychotherapists to offer a community gathering that we titled "The Crones Are In," lightning struck. The word "crone" shocked friends and family, sending them fleeing for their dictionaries. Close women friends, several years older than I, expressed their dismay at my apparent carelessness of language. The women in my family openly opposed such radicalism. Both groups wrote postcards and letters containing definitions from their esteemed dictionaries, chastising me for my ignorance. The consensus from the collections that I received seemed to cluster around the image of a crone being, at best, an ugly, withered old woman, and, at the lower end of the continuum, very closely aligned with witches—a ferocious, terrifying, powerful old woman perhaps capable of casting evil spells and devouring children. I peered into the mirror, refrained from asking "Am I the fairest in all the land," and instead studied the sprinkling of small, stubby, stiff white hairs poking out of my chin, a few gathering above my top lip, but not quite reaching my nose. Not yet, anyway. A hag? On the way to being a witch? Or simply a woman who explored the possibilities of acknowledging the wisdom accumulated during more than five decades of marching out to embrace life fully?

On Winter Solstice 1995 we opened the doors to a cavernous, mostly unheated room in the Women's Center in our town, and the women came. We were amazed when women of all ages arrived; they were from twenty to eighty years old, and, to our surprise, the majority were under forty. We discovered they were excited about hearing our viewpoints and eager to share their own. We had planned which of us would conduct each of four segments we had identified as our structure: the opening and greeting; a ritual, which took the form of a reading; the invitation for questions and discussion; and a closing ceremony.

Each woman, as she entered the room, was personally welcomed; we noted the parts of the word, "well" and "come." "It is well that you have come," intoned Dame Virginia as she greeted the women.

Once everyone was seated, Dame Ginger began by introducing herself with that title: "I am Dame Ginger, the mistress of my own household and my office." We were each introduced in the same manner. Dame Ginger shared her definition of "crone," using Walker's subtitle: "a woman of age, wisdom and power." A few years earlier, Dame Ginger had entered cronehood by giving a "Pause

Party" for herself and her friends; to mark her entry into menopause she served Bloody Marys as the beverage of the evening, following a suggestion by her older sister.

The four of us formed a four-cornered figure, representing the four points on the compass. We read from Duerk's book in turn. We moved into a semicircle and faced the larger circle of women across from us, who had joined us on the longest night of the year. Where I live, winter wraps everything in darkness; nights come early, leaving behind solemn days, gray and sodden, which require a joining together to keep bones warm. That Winter Solstice evening, without saying anything to one another, the four of us showed up in black and gray-toned clothes, matching the season. Our inner fires penetrated the dark, cold room as our faces peered out from beneath shawls and hats. The light of a single candle reflected in our eyes as we settled back to listen to any questions the women asked of us.

When the first woman stated her question, we invited her to come sit with us in our smaller circle. We had piled pillows for the questioner to seat herself in comfort. We listened. Then, when she was finished, we answered with what was real and true for us, beginning with the oldest crone, Dame Georgia, and ending with our most junior crone, Dame Virginia. We made space for the richness of spontaneity. We strove to be responsible to the women who gathered, and to ourselves as well. The diversity among us filled the space. We spoke as crones, not as therapists. Dame Georgia likes to describe our "Crones Are In" gatherings as authentic and pure offerings to ourselves and the women who join us. From the first, we all felt a great sense of history, as we looked out at the lovely faces of young women, and women our own ages, their faces lined with living and gathering knowledge. We knew we had joined the heritage of older women who were able to provide counsel throughout the ages.

We listened as women spoke of relationship, childbearing, loss and grief, illness and death. The language came from the hearts of the questioners, and was heard in the hearts of the listeners.

Well nourished and warmed by our being together, we closed the circle by giving each woman a small candle, which each in turn lighted from the one central candle which glowed all evening. The darkness was lifted by the light pouring over all of us, as we silently made a promise to ourselves to protect, honor, and love ourselves in the winter ahead. We marked the time as a period of hibernation and the quiet nurturing of our hopes and desires. We promised to meet again on the vernal equinox.

As each season shifted, the "Crones Are In" showed up. We dressed in seasonal costume. We created an archway reflecting the season's symbols. Women passed through the archway and were greeted by one of us as they entered. "Welcome. It is well that you have come." The numbers of women attending grew. Each time we met, we followed the same format, realizing that we had fashioned a ritual that offered comfort and containment for those who joined with us. We recognized that ritual grounded and focused the event. Ritual helped us create a contained space which provided a home for inspiration to visit, where transcendence could occur, and where healing could take place.

After the Summer Solstice planning session, the four of us became aware that the time of harvest, the autumnal equinox, would follow a busy, abundant summer. We concluded that it was time for us to gather ourselves in from the fields where we had been busy planting and growing. We decided to have a weekend retreat on a rugged, wild part of the coast for our next crone event. It was our time for renewal and reassessment, so we would be ready for that all-important season of winter. When we announced to the women who came to the Summer Solstice session that we would be tending to our own well-being come fall, returning to celebrate our first year of doing the "Crones Are In" on Winter Solstice, many women sighed. Disappointment crowded in. A woman who traveled a distance to meet with us thanked us for setting an example of gathering in, and of how to do it. The tone shifted, and women began to talk of how hard it is to give to oneself. The crones crowed their delight at having again listened to the small quiet voice of intuition, which, after all, was the creative spark that had been inside each of us when we first crafted the "Crones Are In" series. That night, Summer Solstice, the sun stayed high for many hours, allowing us time to see each other clearly and to rejoice in what we had done. We liked what we saw.

Darkness doesn't really happen in the summer, this far north. A quiet settles over the land for a few short hours, giving a small rest to the creatures living here. Morning floods the damp earth early and the new day begins. The crones are now in summer, listening for intuition to whisper, for creativity to emerge between us. We will wait to see what is growing. We will be ready to gather our new harvest.

MEREDITH JORDAN AND
ELEANOR MERCER

Meredith Jordan, M.A. is a Licensed Clinical Professional Counselor in private practice in Saco, Maine. She works with individuals, couples and groups on issues of psychospiritual development, change and loss, illness and wellness, and recovery from abuse. She is fifty-three and the mother of an adult daughter and son.

Ellie Mercer, M.Div., is Minister of Faith Education at First Parish Church in Saco, Maine. She has served as associate minister in several large churches in Maine and Massachusetts, and as chaplain and counselor in private secondary schools. Now fifty-nine, she has a private practice in spiritual direction where she works with individuals and couples who are questing and questioning the place of the Sacred in their lives. Ellie is the life partner of Peter, and mother of two grown sons.

Both women are lifelong activists and advocates of social justice. They have learned from their own spiritual journeys that each of us is born encoded with a divine blueprint, and that our most important task through life is to bring that blueprint into full expression. Their Web site is www.rogersmckay.org.

Prayers for Change

We might never have met had it not been for a moment of synchronicity arranged for us somewhere in the heavens. Ellie had just accepted the call to be the associate minister in a church to which I was reluctantly being dragged by a friend who was tired of my whining about being "spiritually bereft." Hearing Ellie preach that morning, in her first sermon at this church, awakened my longing for strong, courageous women with whom to be in deep counsel about matters of the spirit. I left the service that day with an appointment to talk further with this woman minister, who laughed like no one I had ever known before, or have ever known since.

The day of our appointment, I had a panic attack in the parking lot. It seemed inconceivable to me, given the eclectic nature of my personal and spiritual journey, that we would be able to find common ground; but, without regard for my hesitations, some invisible force propelled me into this first conversation. I had promised myself that I would not even climb the stairs to her office unless I was willing to tell the truth of who I am. I was determined to know if there could be a place in any circle of worship for a woman like me, who had traveled a path that led me through many faith traditions before finally reaching an understanding and experience of the Sacred that felt true all the way to my bones. When I finished the telling of my story, I asked her this question: Is there a place here for someone like me?

Ellie never hesitated in her response. She said: If there isn't a place for you here, then there isn't a place for me, either.

The conversation that was born between us in that instant has never stopped. Our two paths, so different that it's almost as though the differences were choreographed to create an explosion of creative potential at the moment we'd meet, intersected at that time and place—where a woman theologian and a woman psychotherapist were each hard-questioning the missing elements of their respective lives and professions. We both dared immediately to hold each other's feet to the fire, and we could sense that bright, energetic sparks flew when we asked, really meaning it: Who are you? And when we listened, as each of us answered the other from the depths of her unmet longing.

Within a year, we'd gathered other women around us who wanted to join us in these conversations. Within two years, we were offering our first groups in spiritual exploration, which we called "Deepening in the Spirit for Women." We had been listening to the voices of male spiritual authority, and following spiritual or religious paradigms that had been created and perpetuated primarily by men, for so many years, that—for a time—we wanted to hear only the voices and songs of women seekers; the stories, dreams and myths of women's spiritual journeys; the lessons and wisdom women had gleaned from the rich, fertile earth of the joys and sorrows in their lives.

In our third year of friendship and collaboration, we incorporated as a nonprofit, multifaith educational organization dedicated to providing spiritual direction for all seekers, and we expanded our range of programs. Late one afternoon, as we searched for a name for this fledgling organization, Ellie's husband, Peter, wandered through the conversation at a critical moment. Hearing our struggle to find a name that truly suited the work we were doing, he proposed our mothers' birth names. Ellie's mother, who died of untreated breast cancer when Ellie was twenty-four, and my seventy-five-year-old mother, who struggles to breathe every day as the result of a life-threatening lung disease, were our first spiritual guides and mentors. Like so many women who lived quiet, faithful lives of service to their families and communities, they had never been acknowledged or honored for their contributions to the lives of people around them. This was our chance to correct that injustice. From that day forward, we became Rogers McKay, after Berta Rogers Sager and Beatrice McKay Harmon.

Today, our groups include both women and men, and address a broad range of issues being considered by faithful seekers of many spiritual traditions. Among our ongoing groups is a dream circle of midlife women, ages forty-two to sixty-nine, who have been meeting for two years to share their dreams and dream insights with one another. Together, the women of this group probe their dreams for recurring themes of a re-emerging Feminine consciousness; themes of building new structures and forms which reflect that consciousness;

themes of birthing relationships of equality and true partnership. Though the women in this group often balance full-time professional lives with family responsibilities or the burdens of graduate school, this group is so filled with laughter, compassion, wisdom, love, and acceptance of the journey toward spiritual eldering that none of us would miss it! Our dreams tell truths that sometimes make us squirm in embarrassment or discomfort, but they always expand the range and richness of our inner lives.

In our first two years as a nonprofit organization, we struggled to find ways to fund this work. Like so many worthy groups of people doing good work in the world, we tried to match ourselves to those funding sources that seemed to share our particular focus on women's spiritual issues and journeys. There weren't many. A full year of back-breaking grant writing attracted some interest to our work but no hard funding. It was all too clear to us that we would fit the guidelines of these large philanthropic organizations only if we altered our purpose or our language—to sound more religiously conservative, or more secular, or to fit the comfort levels of the particular funding source— which we not were willing to do.

Operating out of the wild courage that comes with age and whispers—sometimes shouts—we refused to be chameleons in the funding process, to conform to anyone or anything but who we most authentically are. We had worked long and hard to remember how to speak in what we had come to call our native tongue—or essen-tial nature—and were not about to sacrifice it now. This brave con-viction gained us points for integrity but left the bank balance hovering near zero.

In a moment of desperation, as we were brainstorming ways to fund ourselves that were congruent with our focus on spiritual direction and our principles of authenticity, the idea for "Prayers for Change" was born to Laura Read—pilot, entrepreneur, hospice pioneer, mother, partner, and, much to our great good luck, one of our most faithful supporters. The beauty of the Prayers for Change project lies in its reciprocity, wherein every participant gives and every participant receives. All the while, we join together in serving a greater good.

Prayers for Change is an innovative pilot project, and we could not have created it without the help of gifted artist and potter Nancy Read (no relation to Laura), who made twenty-four beautiful clay pots—of teal green, blue, lavender, and rose colors—each with the words "Prayers for Change" inscribed on its face. Every participant in the program chooses a pot, which is then on loan to them for a year.

Once a week, Ellie and I sit down to compose a letter on matters of local, national, and world concern or celebration which need our personal and collective prayers. These issues run a gamut, from nonviolent resistance to threats or actions of war, to environmental concerns, to world hunger needs. We add to these concerns requests for prayers for individual people who are in need or crisis, and send the letters via e-mail (and a few by snail mail) to all members of the PFC circle. In turn, each one of them makes a commitment to set aside time daily to pray for the people and the issues mentioned in the letter. They may also request prayers at any time, so the process is truly circular in nature.

Each time they pray, they empty their wallets or pockets of all silver change, which goes into the clay pot and collects there—until we meet, four times each year, for a whole-group prayer gathering. At those times, in rituals of song and storytelling, we empty the pots. The money that is collected from the pots goes directly into a scholarship fund and enables us to provide both individual and group spiritual direction work to all who seek it, regardless of their ability to pay. This practice supports our commitment to a policy of economic justice and allows us to live true to our consciences. There need be no lies, modifications, or distortions of who we are, and what we do, in order to develop and draw financial support for the work we offer—work which seeks to free and feed the hearts and the spirits of all people who wish to live authentic, Spirit-centered lives.

We are incredibly blessed to do what we do, and we know this. We work from a foundation of friendship which has encouraged us, empowered us, and just as often challenged both of us to step up to the plate as women elders and wisdom keepers in this culture. And our friendship is a significant ingredient in what makes all of this tick. What we encourage the participants in our groups to do—to explore their own inner lives—we do with each other. Our work week begins with lit candles and a heart council with each other, where we explore our own dreams, intuitions, and the many ways in which the Mystery is at work in our midst.

It is, blessedly, an honor to have a friend to whom one can entrust her dreams, however clear or obscure or confounding or demanding they may be (and they often are all of that). Neither of us takes this gift of friendship for granted. Early in our collaborative partnership, when Ellie was just beginning to remember the sound of her own words forming low in her throat, she had a profound dream in which she saw herself in a black velvet hat, dancing her own unique dance. The next Christmas, purely by serendipity, I found her that black velvet dancing hat! In this and so many other ways—through laughter, through tears, through the painstaking formation of a theology of women's faithfulness and courage—we have called each other into the full, strong inhabitation of her life. As we call ourselves, so too do we call others to the sacred task of living a fully inhabited, fully honorable, and fully expressive life in the Spirit.

Working side by side, we create a body of work which we are lucky to love and which helps others to learn—or to remember—their own native tongues. We sometimes refer to this as the "blueprint" or "code" with which we are inseminated at the time of our birth. Each one of us is unique, and each one of us is needed to fulfill a part of the greater plan. We are assured and re-assured that this work ripples out in both small and large waves to touch the hearts and lives of many children and adults—because we see the results each day. We live and work at what we call the theological cutting edge, where heart and spirit come together in a burst and bloom of authentic knowing which gifts not only our individual lives, but our friendships, families, communities, and the world in which we live. What greater blessing can there be, than to spend one's precious life energy and accumulation of hard-earned wisdom in this way!

YONAH KLEM

Yonah Klem has been attracted to many things, and has pursued them. She married before finishing college and had three children by the time she was twenty-six. Five years later, inspired by a stint on the local planning commission, she earned a master's degree in public administration. After being a serious dance student as a child, and again as an adult, a particularly interesting movement workshop led her to a career as a dance-movement therapist, and a doctorate in counseling. Her most recent venture has been to start a three-year training program for teachers of Jewish meditation. She maintains a small private practice, with a speciality in treating people who have endured trauma, and she studies and teaches meditation and yoga. She is still married to her best friend. And she weaves beads every chance she gets.

Bitten by a Beady Bug

Of course it was all the fault of Clarissa Pinkola Estes. I was reading her book, *Women Who Run with the Wolves*, when I came across a sentence about doll making. I don't remember what gave me pause just then. Never in my fifty years before encountering that sentence had I considered doll making. Knitting was the primary craft in which I had any interest or skill, and that was modest on both counts. I knew very little about sewing and did not care to learn more. Even so, doll making suddenly seemed fascinating.

When my mother died, a few years before my encounter with Estes, I inherited a sizeable collection of her craft materials. Nobody else wanted them, so I claimed them almost as an afterthought. It was into this treasure horde that I went digging for stuff—fabric, beads, anything with which I could make a doll. My first effort was a sock stuffed with laundry lint, embellished with beads for face and features, and fantastic multicolored yarn for hair. Even though fairly small, she was a ferocious goddess of anger.

I liked the process and I liked the results. Over the next year or so I made about a dozen more dolls, goddesses I called them, icons of the energies or ideas I was interested in at the moment. They were all made out of found materials, and embellished with beads in one way or another. After a lifetime of more academic pursuits, I liked the idea of developing a craft, an art form, something not remotely intellectual or scholarly.

My ideas soon ran into the wall of my lack of basic skills. I couldn't figure out how to make arms that would stay in place while I clothed them. I made a great face, lavishly detailed with beaded embroidery, but couldn't fashion a body to hold it. My usual approach when confronted with ignorance about something is to look for a book; but none of the ones I found dealt with how to create doll sculptures. My second approach is to look for a class. That is how I came to be looking through the catalog of the Split Rock Summer Arts Program at the University of Minnesota, which someone had suggested as a possible place to find a doll-making workshop.

It was not. Instead there were four or five classes in bead weaving. Playing with beads had been one of the best parts of making dolls. The sparkle and color of the tiny bits of glass were delightful, especially under bright light and magnification. Dolls were immediately put aside.

I called the program offices to see if any of the classes would be suitable for someone like me who had so little knowledge or skill with beads. I was told that the loom-weaving class would be fine for beginners, so off I went.

The class was like being in an anteroom of heaven. We were to meet from nine to five every day for a week. In fact, we were there well before nine and usually stayed long past dark, weaving beads. At night we dreamt of beads. Among ourselves, we talked about almost nothing else but beads. By the end of the week I barely knew what my tablemate did in the rest of her life.

Our instructors suggested that we do a small project. Never having woven beads on a loom, or off, I had no idea how time-consuming the process was. Picking up each bead is a separate motion. Mistakes almost always require that the thread be pulled out of the needle so that some beads can be removed and others replaced. At first, because the eye of the needle is so small, it was taking ten minutes just to rethread the needle every time I made a mistake. I made a beaded doll, with warp thread for hair, embellished with beaded fringe. More than four years later, it remains the most ambitious project I have done.

Working on that doll was more than ambitious. I loved bead weaving even more than doll making. I loved the repetitious movement. I loved the attention to detail. I loved getting efficient enough to thread the needle in ten seconds. I loved getting sophisticated enough to appreciate the differences between Czech beads and the bigger-holed Japanese ones. I loved how my creativity and skill grew as I practiced and experimented and took more classes at Split Rock.

The only real downside to bead weaving is that it is easily the most sedentary occupation I have ever tried, requiring even less body movement than moving a pen across a piece of paper. I, who knew myself to be one of the most impatient people on the planet, now had patience beyond what my poor aging body could tolerate. Despite reminding myself to get up and stretch, I let myself get sucked into the "just-one-more-stitch (or row, or bead, or something)" routine, until my shoulders ached and my legs were so stiff I could barely stand when I finally got up. My newfound ability to sit still was, and remains, a constant amazement to me and to anyone close enough to know what a flittery person I really am.

Bitten by a beady bug, was I.

Perhaps what I loved most of all was hearing people whose opinions I respect refer to me as an artist. I am musically talented, and intellectually competent enough to have earned several advanced degrees. When I first encountered bead weaving I had been a mental-health counselor for more than fifteen years. For all of the study that goes into doing that work well, I know that counseling is also intuitive, an art as well as a science. I am good at it.

The word "artist," however, always brings to my mind someone who works with her hands, one who paints or carves, or coils clay, or molds or models or weaves. Handwork. Art as the work of one's hands and eyes, intellectually informed perhaps, but more of the heart than the head. My ability to carry a tune does not seem to me to be an art, no matter how accurate my pitch is, perhaps because I haven't put much effort into developing this talent. Counseling, for all of its intuitive requirements, is too intellectual to be considered only an art. Bead weaving, however, fits my criteria. My designs are interesting and beautiful and skillful enough that other people call them art.

I recently sold my first piece, a red beaded bag full of ridges and ruffles, delicate and bright.

"Artist" is what I am called sometimes. The thought that I am more than merely skillful, especially with my hands, makes me giggle with delight, even now that it is no longer such a novel idea.

I don't make dolls anymore, although I may again someday. I don't run with wolves, either. However, if running with wolves is understood as noticing what grabs my heart and letting it carry me along past countries unexplored to destinations barely imagined, then the art of bead weaving is the wildest thing I have ever done.

Clarissa Pinkola Estes, masterful storyteller that she is, is to blame for all of this unexpected change in the story of my life. Would I have gotten to this happy place without finding that particular sentence in that particular book, which arrived before me just as I was ready to read it? I have no idea. She pointed out a way and I took it. Wandering this way and that, I found an artist in me, and a patient one at that.

JOAN LEMIEUX

*During her twenty years of teaching high school and college,
Joan LeMieux became a freelance writer for a number of
magazines and papers and co-authored a local travel book.
After leaving teaching, she owned a small advertising/public
relations firm, worked in tourism both regionally and state-wide,
worked in hospital administration, and was elected as a county
commissioner. Having been a mother of three, a widow at fifty,
remarrying at sixty-one, and engaged in this wide variety
of occupations, Joan is a woman who is willing to step off cliffs
and fly. She likes to beckon other women to go with her.*

Women Navigators

In the 1700s, a ship's captain turning the wheel with sails billowing in the wind knew he was entering uncharted waters once he lost sight of the familiar shores and headed out to open ocean. Navigators did not have the calculated knowledge of longitude necessary either to identify exactly where they were, or to tell them how to get to destinations they hoped to reach.

Enter the *rutter*, described in James Clavell's novel *Shogun* as "... a small book containing the detailed observation of a pilot *who has been there before* ... it set down the how we got there and *how we got back* ... everything necessary for a safe voyage. It told of wind patterns, what to expect of the currents, the names of storms and the times of fair winds. It listed the shoals, reefs, tides, heavens." For the royal houses and major trading companies financing both the search for treasures in the New World and the extension of their empires, getting the ships there, and back (a vital part of the plan, mind you) required the fastest, cheapest, and most reliable passage. Obviously these *rutters* were very valuable, selling for large amounts of money wherever they were available on the market. Often the only way to get them was to steal them.

Why so valuable, or worth stealing? Well, for a current comparison, imagine having access to a major competitor's market plans, along with a listing of major customers and their buying patterns. All the information you need to reach your financial goals for the year. All in one place. Good, detailed charts for reaching important destinations are invaluable.

This knowledge about *rutters* is not just obsolete historical data. There are striking similarities between the experiences of today's women over fifty and the sailors of the 1700s. When women reach midlife, there is the realization that we probably have at least twenty to thirty years left to live, a second adulthood. Losing sight of the receding shores of middle age, we embark on this radically new journey into aging. True, it is a time full of new possibilities. But with this new freedom and a plethora of options it is suddenly a strange and, at times, frightening new place.

Aging is like that—without warning, it's there, and we weren't expecting it. Walking down the street, we see an unknown figure reflected in the store window as we pass by. Who is that? The body changes. Lips lose their boundaries, chins sprout hair . . . surroundings change. Familiar points of reference are gone, friends die, jobs fade into retirement. Golden years turn into tarnished marriages. Parents turn into children. And for the first time, we become aware of our own mortality. Our finite world has edges.

And we ask, "How do we navigate the time that is remaining?" Where are the charts for our major passage? We have no mathematically solid points of longitude and latitude for finding our place in these waters. There are no *rutters* out there for us. We cannot turn to voyages made by our mothers and grandmothers for navigational experience and advice. Their charts are mostly inaccurate now. They did not experience the voyage we encounter today. We are the first generation of women to be given such a long period of time as a "second adulthood." Ours is a time of more freedom, accompanied by greater choices and more decisions. It is a whole new voyage. We are, however, accumulating knowledge and experience as we go. This knowledge can be noted and recorded. We are indeed smack-dab in the middle of a fantastic voyage here and now, and in living color. All sails are up.

Within this group of women today in this midlife voyage is a growing body of experience, "shared experiences to be valued and treasured" (that's the beginning of a *rutter* if ever there was one), for navigating these new uncharted waters.

Listen to a recent gathering of twenty-two women ranging in age from nearly fifty to early seventies. The laughter bubbles up and around the tables full of potluck food, as the women talk of shared experiences. Learning from each other.

"Let me look at your chin again. You say it's a new way to get rid of those black hairs on my chin. Tell me about it."

'Oh, the sweetness of being courted at seventy-one, I adore it."

"My mom is driving me crazy. I can't reason with her. I'm taking the night shift, staying with her now. Been going on for four weeks."

"I almost died when the doctor talked about the rise of AIDS in women over fifty. I figured that at this age I was free to do what I wanted. I thought I knew how to handle this being single at sixty-two. But how in heaven's name do you talk to a man about *that*?"

This is the reality in the second adulthood of many women today. True, a different scenario is out there in society. The accepted "common knowledge" (which is usually a euphemism for either folklore or society's code) is that the pace of life slows down for women in their late fifties, sixties, and seventies. According to these experts, we float in a flaccid backwater, far from the rapids of earlier years. We drift. Our children have left home. We are retiring, or close to retirement. We've settled into our lives, are comfortable, ready to just relax and enjoy the fruits of our age. The financial struggles are fewer, we've got what we need and are no longer striving to get ahead. Our futures are set and safe. We should expect few changes as we settle into aging. Now, obviously, this would hardly be a place to worry about navigational hazards. Reality, rather than society's expectations, however, shows a far different course.

For the women around the table, life is anything but simple and calm. The stories pile up—four cases of breast cancer (all of the women well today), three new houses, one husband dead, three divorces, two separations, one wedding, two firewalkers, two new businesses, one election to political office, one new book started, two new college degrees, new loves, so many retirements, ill and dying parents, young grandchildren needing help, husbands with Parkinson's disease.

This is not lolling on an inner tube in the mill pond. This is active sailing full before the wind on choppy seas and shifting tides. This calls for a good *rutter*, a guide for navigating these waters.

This guide will need to carry the detailed observations of the women who have been there. It will include warnings about what is ahead, where the dangers lurk. Why you must make your decisions, take control of the wheel at this time. Because if you just follow the easy currents of others' decisions, you'll find yourself floundering on the sandbar of someone else's destination.

A woman's decision has got to be, first of all, something that she can live with, and it must be based on where she is right now, not where she planned to be. Nor based on where her husband or her children want or expect her to be. Holding a true course is difficult at this time. The compass for this journey must be accurately calibrated to the True North of our inner selves. We must know who we are and what we need. And sometimes understanding our real needs is very difficult. We will also learn to ignore the course settings that proclaim "young" as a goal and destination. No such journey is possible.

We set our course to determine our own destiny; going back to school, learning a new language, traveling. When being blown off course by outdated expectations from another generation, usually with words such as "You can't do that at your age," or "Good Lord, woman, act your age," it is acceptable to be really angry—pure, good, honest anger. Facing this strong wind instead of just altering our course is necessary at times. But accepting the new course must be our decision. The whine and snivel are merely an albatross around the neck.

You will learn to watch out for wind patterns that caress you with names of "sweet," "quaint," and "perky." They leave your sails no power. Steer clear of "little" in any sentence with "old lady."

Note that these wide, rounded sterns will float again, even after being stranded on outgoing tides of loneliness. Yes, repeated tidal action, the incoming and outgoing wash of fears and joys, laughter and crying, is a natural part of this voyage. Even if you have faced a problem head-on and thought you were finished with it, don't be dismayed if it comes back again and again. This is no measure of defeat. Tidal action, repeated over and over, cleanses the harbors and clears the beaches where we may land.

The geographical landmarks are noted, the hazards of a husband's retirement are marked, the winds of depression about failing health are noted. We incorporate in our *rutter* what we have learned from other women about their journeys. Talk to one woman, and you will learn from at least five women.

Navigators make course corrections when necessary. They do not wait for permission. It's called changing your mind, changing your behavior, changing your future. You notice how someone else negotiated that certain passage between the rocks of anger and guilt in dealing with aging parents, and now you can see a way through, one you had never considered before.

What would a *rutter* look like today? Well, it could look like an e-mail newsletter. Perhaps a weekly edition of "Prune Power" would be a part of it, or a self-published book. The *rutter* could include a renewed retirement network group. As one woman put it, "I need the network more now than ever before. I am more alone, without support now that I no longer work. I'm not talking with my usual women business friends, and I'm having to adjust to a whole new way of life."

Part of a *rutter* might be e-mail or letter contact with a woman isolated at home caring for an aging husband. Take the time to help other women master e-mail, this new communication process. A ribald joke, a small poem, just a cheery hello can be opened up at three in the morning in the silence of our own homes. It's all part of sharing information that will help each of us make the journey easier, better, and more fulfilling.

The *rutters* of the 1700s, showing real experiences of the early captains, altered the way the world was perceived and charted. Other maps made by land-based cartographers were based on imagination, false expectations, misinterpretations, or political intrigue, rather than on actual voyages. More realistic maps and expectations were possible only after the successful voyagers reported what was actually there. So too will the *rutter* of women's voyages change the map of women's roles and expectations in the future. Consider, for example, what will happen when women question the media as to why older women are not on the business pages giving investment advice. Once noted, it becomes a reality. New expectations for older women will come through our lead in navigating these years.

Women changed old expectations and roles when they entered the workplace and moved up to prove their power. Women became school superintendents, airline pilots, CEOs, senators, astronauts. They drive big rigs, ride Harleys. Women can and will do the same thing with aging: redefine outworn roles by living new roles. When we run for office, begin a new career, speak up, note when we need to be included and yell when we are ignored, those women who age after us will have those options accepted by society. When we learn to navigate these hazards in our journey, the charts will show it.

We will model, share, comfort, leave diaries of storms and winds and warnings about shoals of loneliness. There simply isn't anyone else to do this. We are on the journey. We will retell and recount and retain this information, because other women will need it as they pass this way after us. They will use our charts. Their voyages will be easier. And the new charts will change the geography of the world.

DOROTHY BLACKCROW MACK

Dorothy Blackcrow Mack has lived three lives. With her Oberlin B.A., her Yale M.A., and her University of Michigan Ph.D., she enjoyed a successful academic career until she began to feel as if she were in a giant candy store, craving a loaf of bread. With a move to the Pine Ridge Reservation in South Dakota, where she raised a sacred herd of buffalo, survived breast cancer, and lived in a rustic one-room log cabin, she changed her life to embrace the values of extended family, oral culture, the Lakota language, and respect for the Everywhere Spirit. Upon moving to Oregon to be with her ill father, she discovered her own native Molalla roots. She is now a singer for healing ceremonies, a spiritual midwife, and a maker of star quilts. In addition to being a contributing editor to Calyx, *she has won numerous awards for her writing and poetry, and has been published in many literary magazines.*

Si Taeweksin:
Grandmothers Giving Wisdom

I love being a Crone. I even give speeches, "Please Call Me an Old Hag." As Barbara Walker says in *The Crone*, "crone" means "crowned one." And "hag" comes from the Greek *hagia*, or *sacred*. Knowing this, who wouldn't want to claim being a Crone?

When I fill out forms, I don't mark Single (though I am), Married (though I have been, twice), Divorced (though I have been, twice), nor Head of Household (though I am, me and my cat). I make and mark another box: FREE Crone.

My grandson recently said to me, "My rich grandma goes on all these trips, but my poor grandma [who won't buy him video games], you have adventures!" Even with poverty, ill health, and loss, my life is an adventure, for the flower still awaits, not necessarily to be picked, but to be savored for its fragrance.

So what, if our youth-worshipping society has written us off? We're told we are decrepit and powerless, but actually we're just invisible. And because we're invisible, we can do *anything* and no one will notice. Not only can we wear purple, we can wear neon green, hot pink, orange stripes with polka dots, or nothing at all. We don't have to blue our hair and set it in short, tight curls; we can wear it long, loose—or uncut, or in a brush cut, bowl cut, or shaved off completely. We can be outrageous, flaunt ourselves, and demand attention. We can be Maudes and take young lovers. We can go places alone, do what we've always wanted to do, be what we've always wanted to be—now.

But often we don't. For it's hard to believe the opposite of what we've been spoon-fed for years: that older women are pitiful, useless, no-good hags. It helps to be surrounded by others who have chucked off such narrow notions. Crone Circles are one answer.

We need Crone Circles to strengthen ourselves, and to reclaim our rightful roles in society as midwives of both birth and death; as leaders of puberty, marriage, and other ceremonies honoring fecundity and life; as anchors, watchers, guardians, healers, storytellers. We are also Baubo, of the bawdy, wise sexuality. We are roots, tree, mountain; we are the web of the world.

In Crone Circles we can validate ourselves—our existence, our lives, our feelings, our truths. We can share our wisdom and experience. But how can we find each other? We're not likely to find companions in bars, churches, bridge clubs, senior centers (except as the helpers), or inside the covers of *Modern Maturity*.

I found my Crone Circle—*Si Taeweksin: Grandmothers Giving Wisdom*—by belonging to the Red Cedar Circle, which practices *Sisiwis*, or the Sacred Breath native tradition of the Pacific Northwest Coast. Here, native women have always been leaders and healers, and the songs and teachings have survived for thousands of years. This wisdom offers a spiritual framework for the *talking stick circle*, and specific ceremonies led by Crones.

We began *Si Taeweksin* with several different purposes. Some women, scared by menopause, sought role models. Others, professional counselors and caregivers, sought support and renewal. Others simply sought fun with other confessed Crones. But all of us sought the wise-women teachings.

We meet quarterly. We share leadership, each bringing insights from our talents and gifts. After a lifetime of being bossed around by parents, husbands, children, and bosses, it's so relaxing to have no set leader. We are at a time in our lives when we are all leaders. Usually whoever hosts the gathering convenes the circle, and may set a topic.

The *talking circle* is the essence of Crone support. Its structure is both simple and empowering. Whoever holds the talking stick (or feather or stone) has the floor. When finished, she passes to the next until all have had a turn. No one interrupts. Everyone listens with respect. Casual interchange is discouraged. Thus the sharing goes deep.

In the *Si Taeweksin* circles, we follow an ancient practice grounded in thousand-year-old songs and stories. An altar cloth is laid in the center of the floor to focus our attention and concentrate our prayers. A bowl of water and lit candles are all that's necessary, but often women add flowers or sacred objects as well. A woman drums to the Four Directions, calling in the ancestors. Next we sing a water-blessing song, followed by four Sisiwis songs, and the Crone Circle is opened to all present for sharing, from any and all traditions.

Afterward, we may have a dancing circle, but to close the work, we sing another water-blessing song and end with a prayer. Other traditions, such as Wicca, have a similar structure; the details may differ, but the essence is the same.

In our circles, each person contributes her ideas and gifts. We've made our own crowns and worn them in a Croning ceremony; we've anointed one another with Crone oil; we've fashioned Crone images from clay. We've painted our dreams and visions, and written down our personal Winter Counts (a pictographic way of recording the most important events in our lives). We've shared stories from *Women Who Run with the Wolves*—especially that of Butterfly Woman, the wise old dancer, and her native Cowichan counterpart. We've cradled one of our circle in a blanket and gently rocked her, to find that security and love that we once knew and have lost, or needed but never had. We've trusted guided imagery to find an old-age *guardian*. We've played a hilarious game called "Mid-Life Crisis," which is somewhat like Monopoly without a Boardwalk. We've done Tai Chi, Qui Jong, and Sisiwis spring dancing circles. We've bathed in the ocean, in hot springs, and in mountain streams. We've taken sweat together, and held healing circles, brushing off and lighting up one another (with ferns, candles).

We wear loose and flowing caftans. We share good things—herbs, salves, songs, books—and food. We cook luscious meals and eat together. But most important of all, we talk and sing and pray together.

Although so far we've just talked of river rafting, we have taken three weekend trips together, each an exploration of an ancient site. First we went to a red cave on the Oregon coast to become connected with the ocean, the earth, the red paint, and the spiral, and to honor the return of the salmon.

Next we went to see the petroglyph *Tsagaglalal*, "She Who Watches," to feel her power, to sense her place along the cliffs of the Columbia River, and to learn from her directly, to honor her presence and her work. We too are watchers, guardians.

For a Re-naming and Re-birthing ceremony we made a trip to a secluded point above the ocean, near a sea cave and spouting horn. There we honored one of our Crones by covering her and mourning old memories, calling her forth by her new name, passing her between our legs and bathing her new body at a nearby secluded beach. To honor her rebirth and new name, afterward she put on a feast and a giveaway.

Crones are often called upon to do such honoring work, the work of the Grandmothers. Some bring people into the world, choosing the newborns' names; some take people out of the world, singing their names. Some work with young girls, reclaiming the Menstrual ceremonies, and some work with older women, reclaiming the Wise Blood ceremonies. Others are called to the Blessing work: house blessings, office blessings, store blessings, house cleanings, and exorcisms. And there is even work in blessing hot springs and tubs!

We have so many things to reclaim, so many stories and ideas to share, so little time—yet all the time in the world, 6,000 years of time. We can start small. We must remember that we are the roots, the trees, the mountains, the Rock Grandmas who hold the world together.

JOY MITCHELL

As a professional astrologer, writer, teacher, hypnotherapist
and minister, Joy Mitchell has spent over forty years helping
others find their own paths of joy. She has counseled thousands
of clients, lectured, led study groups, appeared on numerous
television shows, hosted the first weekly television series
on astrology in America, and was the co-writer of a popular
astrology book. She has been working on a book titled
Love Ever After: How My Husband Became My Spirit Guide.
Joy lives in Los Angeles, near her son and daughter.

Sexy at Seventy

Who would have guessed that I'd be enjoying the most incredible sex of my life at the age of seventy-two, with a man twenty years my junior? Believe me, it was the last thing I expected.

By the time my husband died in 1995, after eleven years of marriage, my interest in sex had waned to the point where I couldn't even imagine being enthusiastic about "all that nonsense" again. It wasn't a problem, though, because Bob's sex drive had also disappeared as a result of the emphysema that plagued him for the last seven years of his life. But we had a great marriage and a loving relationship, so I was perfectly willing to spend my remaining years in celibacy, even though there were times, I must admit, when I really missed the passion and the romance.

Outside of my roles as housewife and Bob's traveling companion, most of my attention during those years was focused on the interests that had always filled my life as a professional astrologer, teacher, writer, hypnotherapist, and minister. Among other things, I conducted metaphysical workshops and led a weekly study group in Los Angeles affiliated with the Institute of Noetic Sciences, founded by Edgar Mitchell, the Apollo 14 astronaut, after his flight to the moon. Bob always encouraged me in these endeavors, and I loved sharing the wisdom I'd gained through a lifetime of study.

When Bob's death shattered the idyllic scenario of my life, I set about picking up the pieces and putting together a new picture for myself. I've always believed that no matter how great the loss, it is always possible to re-create joy and fulfillment in my life, and usually more than there was before. If it weren't for this belief, I'd never have made it through the deaths of my first two children, my first two husbands, and my only brother. Since it's impossible to stand still, I knew I had to keep growing and expanding or I'd slowly wither and die. Thank God I still had two fantastic children and loyal friends for moral support.

I had lots of choices in front of me after Bob died, and no idea where to start. So I just trusted my instincts and gravitated to the activities I loved, knowing that was the best path to creating a fulfilling new life. I started ballroom dancing for the first time in over a decade. I tried to stay open to new ideas, so when my best friend suggested a trip to Egypt, it sounded exactly like the kind of adventure I was looking for. I'd always been intrigued by ancient mysteries, so I felt that exploring a culture so foreign to my own might inspire me in re-creating my own life. And it did.

I fell in love with Egypt and longed to bring back some of its magic into my new life. I wanted surroundings that reflected the person I was now, rather than my past marriage. So upon returning to Los Angeles, I began redecorating my home to resemble an Egyptian palace. The conventional decor of my marriage was replaced by luxurious ivory furniture and carpets against pale blue walls and billowing curtains, echoing the spacious expanse of sand and sky.

My new bedroom was the pièce de résistance—an ultrafeminine art deco concoction of sheer pink panels swathed against a mauve background that resembled a modern-day harem. My friends gasped in delight and teased me about whom I intended to share my new love nest with. Several of them commented that the room could easily intimidate a man who was not confident in his masculinity, as well as his sexuality. But somehow I had the feeling that the words left unsaid were, "What in the world are you thinking of, at your age? You're too old for sex!"

But I refused to become what the world thinks of as an "older woman." One of my personal secrets for health and happiness is moderation in all things—eating, drinking, exercise, work, and, yes, even sex. But perhaps more important, I surround myself with love and fill my life with as much fun and joy as humanly possible. In fact, when people ask me how I stay so young, I usually tell them it's because I'm happy. It's amazing how well that works! I've also learned not to worry about things I can't change. I take vitamins, but no medications. I've never been overweight and, aside from a cold now and then, I'm exceptionally healthy. I also take pride in my appearance and wear make-up and fashionable clothing. As a result of taking care of myself inside and out, I don't look my age.

So I was far from ready for the old folks' home. And even though I'd been getting senior-citizen discounts for many years (and was often asked for proof), I still believed that romance was possible. I wasn't aware of it at the time, but, looking back, the way I redecorated my bedroom obviously represented my intention to attract love and sex into my life again.

Actually, the man of my dreams was already in my life at that point, but I didn't know it. His name is Jerry, and he'd joined my weekly Noetic Sciences group several months earlier, but obviously I wasn't quite ready for him yet. After one of our meetings, he handed me a Tantric newsletter containing an article he'd written. All I knew about Tantra yoga was that it involved using sexual energy in spiritual ways, but the whole subject was really foreign to me. While reading the newsletter the next day, I noticed an ad for a beginning Tantra workshop, and, I knew I had to take the class.

When I told my friends about it, some were surprised and some were obviously horrified. They couldn't imagine being so adventurous themselves, and I could tell that a few had serious doubts about my sanity. I heard everything from "Aren't you too old for that?" to "You'll probably be the same age as their mothers!"

On one point my friends were right, of course. When I showed up at the workshop, almost everyone in the room was young enough to be my child—and in some cases my grandchild—but it didn't bother me for a minute. I was surprised to see Jerry there, and he was even more surprised to see me. I must admit that I'd always felt attracted to him, but since he was obviously much younger, I ignored the feeling. As I watched him interact with women of his own age that weekend, I just admired him from across the room.

It was the first time we'd been together outside my study group and, as it turned out, that weekend was the beginning of a friendship that would eventually develop into the love of both of our lives.

A few weeks after the Tantra workshop, I decided it was time to attract a new man into my life—not a husband, mind you, just someone to love and have fun with. So I made a list of my top priorities and meditated on them, while imagining the feelings I would experience with this person. The list was short and sweet: someone who loved to dance, who could travel with me, and who was a great lover.

I discovered a long time ago that we ultimately become what we believe. In other words, our beliefs determine what we create in our lives. Most people believe that with age they will automatically lose their health, their strength, their looks, their sex drive, their sex appeal, and their passion. And sure enough, their beliefs are usually confirmed. As a culture, we tend to react to the idea of older people having sex with everything from surprise to shock to disgust. This is probably because our parents taught us from an early age that sex is dirty, so how could they possibly be doing anything like that at their age! After all, when their passions had cooled, why wouldn't they be able to control themselves.

But I'd always held beliefs that were unconventional, and in this case I decided to create a different experience of aging—my own experience. I may not be interested in the same things that fascinated me at thirty-five, but it's not because "I'm too old." It's more like "been there, done that." I'm convinced that one of the primary keys to staying young is learning new things.

About a month later, Jerry and I suddenly realized we were more than friends. We were in love. And he was far more than I had asked for. Not only did he like to dance, he was a writer who could travel whenever he pleased. And it didn't take long to discover he was also the most amazing lover I'd ever had. On top of that, he was highly intelligent, sensitive, generous, creative, and drawn to all the metaphysical subjects that fascinated me. I shudder to think what I would have missed if I'd listened to all those voices warning me about the workshop, insinuating that I was too old for sex or that our age difference would never work.

Now I'm enjoying the most romantic relationship I've ever known, with a tall, handsome, sensitive man who possesses a boundless imagination and makes me feel like a goddess. He also feels right at home in my bedroom! We aren't married, nor do we live together, but Jerry bought a townhouse five minutes away and usually spends four or five nights a week at my condo. This way we have our own homes, our privacy when we want it, and our own space to write and create, which works out perfectly for us. It also keeps the romance alive.

But the truly remarkable part of our relationship is our sex life, which is on a whole different level than anything I've ever experienced. From Jerry's Tantra training, he's taught me how to prolong sensual pleasure so that the journey becomes even more important and memorable than the destination. I've learned that the five senses—taste, touch, smell, sight, and hearing—hold an unlimited cornucopia of physical, mental, and emotional delights. And we use them all: flowers and incense; dancing in flowing veils, jeweled collars and headdresses; exquisite caresses with fur, feathers, and velvet; the sounds of a waterfall or the ocean on a moonlit night; the stirring rhythms of African drums and Middle Eastern music; the natural sounds of our own pleasure and verbal expressions of love. I've learned to create emotional intimacy through eye contact, and to give and receive the magical energy of love between our bodies.

In the past three years, I've had a lot of experiences which aren't unusual in themselves, but some might consider them pretty far out at my age: attending Tantra yoga workshops; snorkeling nude with eight people in the Caribbean; belly dancing with a seven-foot python; parasailing in Catalina; enjoying swing and salsa dancing; attending rock concerts; making love on the beach in Cancún, in a swinging bed, in the hammock on my patio by moonlight, and in bubble baths by candlelight. Talk about romantic!

What a difference from my earlier sex life! Looking back, I can see my own progress, beginning with an incredibly advanced mother who told me sex was beautiful . . . but only when you were married. So I was a virgin when I married at nineteen, as most of us were back then. And sex was a brand-new adventure that I couldn't wait to explore. But it seemed to be only about reaching orgasm. I didn't have a clue about how to create intimacy or establish a strong emotional bond between myself and a partner. I just allowed my physical body to take over and eventually climax.

Now, don't get me wrong; I've had plenty of great sex in my life, but more recently I've discovered that it offers amazing physical, mental, and emotional benefits that most people aren't aware of.

For example, sex keeps me younger. As long as my sexual fires are burning, I feel as vital as I did in my prime. Actually, sex is the original Fountain of Youth. I've also found that being adored by a loving partner is as life-enhancing as a magic elixir . . . and makes age totally irrelevant.

Sex makes me physically healthier. In fact, it literally regenerates my body. Not only does my skin stay smoother and my body more relaxed, but I'll bet that when they lay me to rest, I'll still have all my sex organs intact. You know what they say—"Use it or lose it." Science has proven that infants who aren't touched usually don't survive, and that older people wither and die faster without the life-preserving energy of physical contact.

In addition to giving me a more youthful and healthy body, sex boosts my self-esteem and emotional well-being. My partner's expressions of love and admiration feel wonderful, but my own loving feelings in response are the greatest nourishment of all. Perhaps some day science will document how psychologically therapeutic a healthy sex life can be.

Finally, sex not only regenerates me physically and emotionally, it renews me spiritually as well. Since I consider sex to be sacred, I've found that making love elevates my consciousness to a higher state, where I'm in touch with my spirit or soul. For me, it's similar to a religious experience.

But the most important thing I've learned about sex at seventy-two is that it's never too late . . . and it even gets better with age!

SUSAN PERCY

Susan Percy is a writer and editor whose work has appeared in Redbook, Glamour, Reader's Digest, Southern Accents, America West, USA Today, *and* Atlanta Magazine. *She has been honored by the Society for Professional Journalists for her editorial writing. She is Director of Communications for Paideia School in Atlanta, where she lives with her husband, writer Paul Hemphill. Her daughter, Martha, attends American University.*

Girl Groups in Graceland

In or out of a pinch, I'll take Lucy and Ethel over Butch Cassidy and Sundance any day. I think women do friendship better than men. It certainly seems to be easier for women to interact without a piece of sporting equipment in their hands. And the older we grow, the better we get at friendship, and the more we appreciate the women we share it with.

I've belonged to several different women's groups over the years—typically not Women's Groups, with capital letters and agendas, just groups of women who get together to be together, regularly or semi-regularly. Over the years, there have been new-mothers groups, mothers-of-toddlers groups, women-who-work-together groups, and women-who-used-to-work-together-but-don't-anymore groups.

I have taken to calling them—with a heavy dose of irony, under-stand—"Girl Groups." The phrase calls to mind some of the great six-ties vocal groups we grew up on—the Supremes, the Ronettes, the Shirelles, the Chiffons: lots of hair, lots of attitude and, boy, did it have a good beat, and could you dance to it. Fun undercut with a certain world-weary sophistication, a lot of heart and a lot of toughness.

At present, I hold membership in two Girl Groups, each with four other members. One is made up of women I've known forever—two were grade-school classmates, one I met in college, the fourth I met through the others twenty years ago when we were pregnant with our respective now-college-age daughters. We're all the same age, give or take a year or two. The second Girl Group is made up, with one exception, of people I've gotten to know in the last three years through an advisory board we all serve on for our college. There's a ten-year age span from the oldest (that's me) to the youngest.

Girl Group One gets together every month for dinner and conversation and the occasional birthday observance. We have taken to calling ourselves "The Book Club," even though we aren't and it isn't, just because that requires less explanation. We actually do pass books and book recommendations around, but for the purposes of these get-togethers, girls just wanna have fun. Except for one woman who moved to North Carolina, we all live in or around Atlanta.

Group Two goes by the name "The Committee." The five of us live in three different cities in two different states, so our gatherings are much less frequent. We see one another officially at the twice-a-year meetings of our advisory group, and in between we stay in touch via e-mail or phone. For lunch purposes, two constitutes a quorum. We've treated ourselves to a couple of memorable weekend field trips.

The Committee's most successful weekend jaunt took four of us to Memphis, where we spent an entire day at Graceland, tour headphones in place and cameras snapping, and the rest of the time eating barbecue, listening to music, and buying souvenirs for the families we left behind. It was wonderful fun, but not exactly a weekend of debauchery—by nine o'clock, we were back in our rooms at the No-Name Motel, sipping warm Diet Cokes and watching the Weather Channel. But not before we had a nice long ride through the city with the rental-car speakers blaring early Elvis—"Tutti Frutti," "Heartbreak Hotel," and "Blue Suede Shoes."

The Book Club has been some places, too, but more like weddings and funerals and graduations. In fact, the impetus for instituting our monthly gatherings was the desire to see each other at occasions that don't require pantyhose. We all pretty much know each other's families, and some of us even remember the others' parents when they were the ages we are now. Some of our children went to each other's birthday parties. And among Book Club members, professions or jobs are incidental.

With The Committee, we start with the present and more or less work backward. We met as grownups and professionals—we're all editors, writers, or PR types; none of us knew each other when we were in college, even though we went to the same school. There are spouses and children that we are still getting around to meeting. We use the phone to talk about our work, seek advice, or just vent a little, and we use e-mail to exchange bad jokes and quick greetings.

Both groups run on humor, so I'm going to take a risk. Girl Group humor, by and large, either doesn't translate or else requires so much background explanation that it's rarely worth the effort. But I offer a sample. At the most recent Book Club evening, at Penny's house (I'm changing the names to protect the innocent and the guilty), Penny and Sally, who both grew up in a small town just up the road from Atlanta, were trying, without a great deal of success, to open a bottle of wine. This begged the question, How many nice girls from Lawrenceville does it take to operate a corkscrew? And the answer: Two. One to crumble the cork into the wine, and one to call on the girls from Decatur (Decatur being the small town within metro Atlanta where the rest of us grew up.)

I'd say The Committee's finest hour, humor-wise, came on Beale Street in Memphis, when a friendly German Shepherd attached himself to our group, but that was more of a series of sight gags with no real punch line. I do have pictures, though.

In both groups, of course, it's the personalities that fuel the group chemistry. Maggie serves as The Committee's designated leader. She's the one who snaps open her calendar and says, OK, when? if one of us suggests that we really have to get together soon. She actually looks at road maps and checks gas gauges and calls ahead for hotel reservations.

In The Book Club, Alice is unofficial president and historian. She has total recall of every name and face in our high school graduating class. She remembers fashion faux pas and social mishaps from decades ago. She can describe in excruciating detail the time I left a parked car in neutral in her driveway and we watched it roll down into the woods behind her house. Her mother invited me for dinner because I was too scared to face the music at home, and we all got the giggles at the dinner table, including the highly respectable parents.

Alice and I still fall apart at the mention of "The Fall of the House of Usher." Not the Edgar Allan Poe short story, but the old

B-movie adaptation starring Vincent Price. The two of us, accompanied by Alice's little sister, rode the bus downtown many years ago to Atlanta's old Paramount Theater, long gone now, where we disgraced ourselves with a fit of raucous laughing that almost got us thrown out. As the movie was starting, a girl walking up the aisle of the theater tripped and fell, sending her popcorn high in the air, geyser-like, as she sprawled on the floor. (If this is too subtle, let me help: she fell at *The Fall of the House of Usher*.) I am embarrassed to tell you that it is as funny to me today as it was forty years ago.

Of course, it's not always a laughfest. There's not a sheltered life in either bunch. Our families have lost jobs, faced financial difficulties, survived illness, alcoholism, and depression. Our children have had some tough times. Some of us have seen our parents through decline and death; others are just starting down that slippery slope.

As it happens, I have back-to-back get-togethers with the Girl Groups coming up this week. Thursday night it's my turn to entertain The Book Club, and Friday I'll get in the car and drive to Athens for lunch with three other Committee members.

At the outset, we specifically agreed that the meal is not the point, the getting together is, and that we would dine happily on sandwiches. But we tend to go to some trouble, even though we deny it. (Don't be silly. I just threw this together.) I'm actually looking forward to the trouble part. I've got a couple of days off from work, and there's plenty of time to iron a few napkins, buy some flowers, and find a corkscrew that will satisfy the needs of Lawrenceville and Decatur.

As for Friday, if there's an extra place at the restaurant table, I wouldn't be surprised to find it occupied by a life-size bust of Elvis.

He claimed that place of honor at our last lunch, and his presence had the unmistakable sign of a tradition in the making.

Would I miss either gathering—the Thursday night supper with old friends, or the Friday lunch with new ones? Not a chance.

DEE POTH

Dee Poth's lifelong interest in art and spirituality has guided her through her parenting years and her work as a magazine section editor for a local newspaper, and as a corporate art consultant, to her current involvement in conference and workshop presentations with and for women. Dee speaks about topics such as the feminine face of god, women and the sacred, and goddess mythology. She has written a book, The Goddess Speaks, *now in its second printing. She travels to sacred sites around the world, recently attending a program on the labyrinth at Chartres Cathedral, and has been inspired by gatherings, trips, and rituals with women who share her ideas and passion about women's spirituality.*

Presence of the Goddess

Dappled sunlight danced on the faces of the women gathered in a circle in the great silent room. I stood in circle with them, holding an alabaster jar filled with the oil of the Magdalene: rose, spikenard, and orange. The soft thrump of a drum began to fill the hush. I turned to the woman next to me and held the container of oils to her face so she could inhale the fragrance that was sacred to Mary of Magdala. As the rhythm of the drum held its pace, I put my finger into the oil and carefully placed a drop on my fellow seeker's forehead. I murmured the words of blessing, the cadence of the words blending with the pulse of the drum. As I finished, someone shook a rattle. Its sharp staccato ripple was like the breath of the Goddess sanctifying our ritual. My neighbor turned to the woman next to her, and she, too, softly spoke words of blessing while sharing the sacred oils. And so it went, till each one had blessed one and the circle was complete.

This group of women gathers as fellow seekers of the divine feminine. On a Saturday morning each month, we search for the feminine face of the creative force. We hear stories of the ancient Goddess in all her many manifestations, acknowledge the changing seasons at solstice and equinox time, and celebrate the old holidays: Beltane, Lammas, Samhain. Each person brings an object for the altar that expresses the spirit of the morning to her. She tells the group her name, shows the group what she brought, and explains why this object is significant to her and to the theme of the day. Together we celebrate the gift of the Goddess within.

A keen interest in the spiritual has always been a part of my life. As a young child, I collected what I called "wise sayings." My parents thought it was important to go to church, but in their view each taught the same message, so it did not matter which one I went to. A friend, with whom I had long philosophical discussions, and I embarked on a search to see which set of church doctrines agreed best with our emerging belief systems. We visited the twelve churches in our town and tried to learn a little about each. Eventually we decided we could agree with Martin Luther's ideas. It did not occur to us that there were any religions to consider besides Christianity.

After attending a Lutheran college—and meeting my future husband—I had a brief career in high fashion. When I became a mother, that was my role and I happily devoted myself to it. Through it all, I knew that in my later years I would commit myself to my lifelong interest in art and spirituality. This I have done. When my children were in high school, I went back to work. I began with an interview column on cooking for the community newspaper and went on to become editor of the magazine section. In the eighties, I turned to art and accepted a job with a gallery as a corporate art consultant. Two years later, I started my own consulting business and did this successfully for more than a decade.

During this time, my interests began to focus more and more on my spiritual search. The big questions: Who are we? Where do we come from ? Who is God? Why is he—or *is* he—male? What about a Goddess? were the questions I asked. From this array of queries, my desire to know more about the Goddess and women's spirituality intensified. A friend and I gathered together a group that included a college professor, a financial advisor, a travel writer, a business consultant, and a university vice president. We met regularly for breakfast at someone's house to discuss our bubbling, emerging ideas about goddesses, ritual, and spirituality.

Our first planned event was a llama trek in the Wallowa Mountains. We each designed a ritual to share with the group over the weekend. A year later, we went to a ranch for a weekend of hiking, ceremony, and hot-tubbing. Our regular gatherings lasted more than two years and were the impetus for me to turn to a new direction, both spiritually and in my career.

Each of us prepared something to share with the group to ready us for our first weekend trip. My interest was in the history of the Goddess, the many manifestations of the ancient ones who were recognized as life-givers, death-wielders, and givers of life again. So my offering was a slide show titled "The Goddess Speaks," which addressed the millennia past and the role the Goddess played in those times. From the slide show came the idea of a book, and the result was *The Goddess Speaks* in book form.

I read voraciously about goddesses, and set up a lecture and work-shop with Elinor Gadon, an author whose work I found inspiring. It came together successfully, and out of this event, a friend and I began our Goddess Circle. We invited the women who had attended the workshop to meet with us to discuss the Goddess and to do rituals. Almost all came, and soon we were joined by others. The group has endured for four years now, and it keeps growing as we continue to welcome new members.

There is a hunger in women today to gather together in fellow-ship, to focus on a strengthening and supportive aspect of their spiritual history. That history has been ignored for thousands of years, with the result that women's sense of self-worth eroded until, spiritually, there was little or nothing left. It was felt that women had no history. The absence of a feminine spiritual presence gener-ates a deep-seated lack of confidence and a feeling that there is no connection to the world of our spirit. This can only be corrected with a more complete understanding of our past, and a realization that there was a time when women were honored for their contri-butions to society and to the balance and continuous regeneration of the world. This is one reason there is a proliferation of women's circles. Women gather to explore their past and their future, to cele-brate ancient holidays that recognize the changing seasons, to honor the earth. In groups, women study goddess myths, discuss the idea of ritual, and more important, experience ritual.

In our circle, the format is similar from one meeting to another, but the content is always different. We gather in a circle around a simple altar or focus point. On a cloth of red, there will be candles, perhaps a goddess figure or sea shell, a blessing bowl or meditation card.

We begin with announcements so that everyone will know about relevant local events. A quiet meditation follows, allowing each woman to leave behind the "to do" lists of the week and to be fully present in the moment. This in itself is a refreshing exercise for most of us. After meditation, we go around the circle, and each woman explains what she brought for the altar, and how it relates to the theme of the day. The choice of this object requires a focused moment at home during the week, when the season or the goddess must be considered. Some bring a flower or a stone, perhaps something that suggests a loved family member—a picture, a piece of jewelry—simple objects that are meaningful to the participant. Always there is the feeling that whatever is placed on our altar is blessed through the energy raised by the women present.

Often we embark on a simple craft project that gives us the opportunity to be creative, with no special talents required. What is made is then part of the morning ceremonies. One of us may tell a story about the goddess we honor, sometimes with pictures, often with movement, always with discussion. Some of our members are talented leaders of dance who teach us that our bodies are part of our expression of the spiritual. The purpose of our gatherings is to recognize the powerful interplay of body, mind, and spirit, and to incorporate all of these aspects in our morning.

Ritual can take many forms. It is most effective when no one person is "the Priestess," but when, rather, each participant is recognized as a priestess. When each woman blesses her neighbor with oil or water made sacred by the intent of the group, with words, or with song, she is indeed a priestess. We recognize the sacred center of each woman in the circle.

Though these rituals may be simple, they offer an opportunity to connect with the Earth, with the Great Mother, and with the sacred All That Is. Everyone is both a part of the creation of and a participant in this process, as we gather in circle side by side with like-minded women.

Our mornings end with meditation and a healing circle, during which each person may put in the names of those she would like to be a part of the blessing.

In closing, we always sing together:

> *May Artemis protect you*
> *May Hera provide you*
> *May the woman's soul inside you*
> *Lead you back home.*

I offer this blessing to you as well.

As women growing older, it is important that we recognize that our power to contribute to others does not lessen, but in fact increases. The wisdom we have accrued, the ego needs we have discarded, the opportunity to offer friendship, our self-respect, our acceptance of whatever talents we have, our undiminished ability to learn—and our humble recognition that there is so much yet to learn—are among the blessings of cronedom.

I am, as are so many women today, a seeker of wholeness that can only come with an awareness of the divine. The ancient goddesses who are reemerging in our consciousness are linking us with a past we did not know we have. It is a blessing to gather with women in circles of friendship to learn, to experience, and to make a connection to past and present. We realize that we are part of a continuum of women of like spirit bonding through the ages.

DANA REYNOLDS

For ten years, Dana Reynolds has been facilitating women's spiritual presentations and retreats nationwide. Her background as a visual artist and writer combine to assist women birth their creative gifts in her Spiritual Midwifery workshops and in personalized retreats. As the creator of an artmaking process known as visual prayer, Dana teaches women how to combine ritual with sacred intention through their creation of altars, collage, spirit dolls, and other touchstones. She is the author of Be An Angel, *illustrated by Karen Blesson, and has won awards for her poetry. Articles about Dana have appeared in* D Magazine, Boston Magazine, Lear's, *and the* Dallas Morning News. *A trained labyrinth facilitator, Dana's life follows the spiral path from rim to center and back again. Guiding women to the discovery of their creative inner gifts is the passion that fuels her soul. Her Web site is www.sacredimagination.com.*

Uisual Prayers

It is the eve of a full moon in autumn. Tomorrow night she will shine her brightest, then wane into her slender pose, no less important than her fullness.

The leaf, now wearing the glorious colors of fall's paintbrush, will soon let go of the familiar branch and with a spiral dance to earth begin a transformation from radiant beauty to new purpose and form. These two markings of time, gifted by the moon and changing seasons, mirror my present foothold on the mysterious labyrinth of life.

I too am nearing my fullness. It is a moment in time, not unlike the hour before the leaf separates from the tree, when everything is vibrant, colorful, exquisite. Grace and fruition coexist.

Fifty-two calendar years spell my age. The cells deep in the fibers of my psyche, body, and soul whisper to me in ancient languages from the place of dreams: "You are ageless. You carry your story and the stories of women throughout time. Your wisdom is sacred; it is women's wisdom. Remember the gifts you were given to share."

I believe this is a universal message for the women of our generation. We are being called to remember our gifts of creativity. We have
the potential to pour ecstatic beauty into our lives from the ancient
well of feminine knowing. Our creations will reflect to others their
unique creative gifts, while offering them healing. Each exquisite gesture of expression ignites another's point of inspiration. Sewing quilts
and making spirit dolls, writing poetry, forming collage from our
prayers, creating altars as places of devotion—we, with these sacred
practices, become our wise women's spiritual language.

As I sit in circles with women coming of age, women who have
gathered from various places on the map, there is often a theme, a
golden thread, running through the shared stories. It is the thread of
remembering, the way the moon and the leaf remember their purposes. We are remembering who we are—a family of women experiencing the voices and visions of a collective dream. This universal
revelation has a singular purpose. It is unmasked to each of us according to our unique ways of understanding. The strange repeated message, composed of symbols, signs, and urgings, is simply: "Remember
your gifts, and share them with one another." It is through this
remembering that we grow wiser.

Collectively we are remembering, both consciously and uncon-
sciously, that we are spiritual midwives. Each of us has the potential to
birth herself into the full expression of her creative gifts and healing
wisdom. This birth brings us to our centers, to reclaim the knowledge
we have been given to share with others through our offerings of
imagination and inventiveness. Spiritual midwives are mentors, healers, and artists. Through reflection, ritual, art making, and journaling,

we craft our stories into tangible form and place them on the altars in the centers of our circles. The spiritual midwife incorporates beauty and sacredness into everyday living for herself and for others.

Priscilla's broken heart is healing. She feels ready to beckon a new love relationship into her life. With this intention she is inspired to prayerfully choose touchstones and placement for an altar to call forth passion and partnering. Her choice of setting is atop an antique chest of drawers in her bedroom. A postcard depicting a timeless Rodin sculpture of two lovers entwined is her first offering. The woman in the image reminds Priscilla of herself. She places the postcard in a gold frame to give it the importance it deserves. A tiny crystal rosary is tenderly hung on this icon as a blessing of her intention to both embrace and be embraced. Two pink roses, the color of the heart chakra, are arranged in a small bud vase and placed nearby. Pictures of the Blessed Mother from Mexico and Russia invoke the Divine Feminine's intercession for her prayers. As a final gesture, Priscilla lights a ylang ylang and patchouli-scented candle, representing sensuality. Her altar is a visual prayer affirming that love, passion, and meaningful relationship are being invited to share her life and her healing, open heart. Eventually, Priscilla's gift of knowing how to arrange furnishings with sacred intention leads her to begin a new business. She now shares her intuitive understanding to help others clear their living spaces to restore tranquillity to their lives. Order and flow are the result.

Our natural world demonstrates these principles. Nature stimulates our metaphorical birthing process through our senses. The moon blesses us with her light, and her radiance awakens our dreams and visions; the autumn leaves provide a palette of color for our eyes. Their rustling song, accompanied by the afternoon breeze, is the song of creation. Beauty and inspiration thrive in the natural world, beckoning the muse and providing fresh kindling for our creative fires. Each new season and the ever-changing landscape of the night sky offer gifts to stir and awaken our creative imaginings.

Lee lovingly crafts a small doll with a white clay face. She fashions a body of blue fabric printed with gold stars and moons, carefully stuffing her with cotton batting and motherly love. This visual prayer has been created for her young daughter, Emily, to represent her mother's devotion to her. Lee is away on retreat, and she will present it to Emily when they're reunited. Her visual prayer holds the message that even when they are apart, they are connected by their love.

Through my work as a facilitator of women's spiritual retreats, I have been transported deep into mystery while witnessing women, like Lee, as they birth their stories into tangible form through sacred art making. These soulful creations are actually visual prayers.

Visual prayers are born from holy intention and devotional awareness in varied forms of expression as imaginative and diverse as the situations that call them forth. The remarkable women who find themselves compelled to consciously create altars, spirit dolls, collages, handmade books and journals, quilts, and wearable art, do not refer to themselves as artists. Most of them have always felt intimidated by the idea of making art. However, women who are moving into the later years of life often are infused with newfound courage. The old internal voices that have been negating desires to be daring and spontaneous are suddenly growing faint. A strong, clear voice emerges, to encourage and guide with assurance. This is the voice of the creative spirit.

One October afternoon, Susan receives guidance and inspiration from the depths of her soul. She begins to choreograph a special winter's holiday experience for her parents, husband, and two grown children. Her mother and father have been divorced since she was a teenager and have remained close friends throughout the years. Susan somehow senses time is slipping away. Planning a reunion for the people she loves most in the world becomes more than just a passing thought. It is a clear calling. She finds the perfect setting, a warmly furnished farmhouse in the Texas hill country. In the days before the reunion, her own kitchen becomes a place of transformation while she prepares all of the family's favorite foods to take to the farmhouse. Susan follows her intuitive guidance and creates countless special touches. Holiday decorations, meaningful music, creative surprises—everything is perfection. The reunion becomes an unforgettable time, blessed with laughter and celebration.

When they return home, Susan loses herself in artistic alchemy. She lovingly makes handmade memory books for her mother and father, filled with photographs and quotes from their cherished holiday.

Soon after this sacred time, her father becomes ill. The little book of photos transforms into a focal point on one of the many altars she creates in his home while he is dying.

Five months after her father's death, her mother follows. The country holiday that had been a living visual prayer to Susan's family is suspended in time within the pages of her little memory books. Her feminine gift of knowing this would be a final joyful gathering called forth her gifts, and she delivered them with love and caring—the same love and caring she shared with her parents till the last.

Magic happens when a circle of women tenderly place their stories of the heart, like Susan's, into the center. We midwife one another into a discovery process that runs like a river carrying us back to our authentic natures. There is dancing and mask making. Prayer beads are strung as meditation. Tiny goddesses are made from rich red clay. Handcrafted paper is folded into a book that is carefully rubber-stamped to tell a story without words. Flowers are woven into garlands and crowns. Each creation inspires another's process of imagining and inventing.

Through our crafts we return to the ancient wisdom, as our hands and hearts work in unison to reveal the beauty and knowledge we have been carrying within us all along. And so, one by one, we tell our stories through our visual prayers. We make an altar to honor a healed heart, stitch reassurance into a spirit doll, craft a book of memories, or cut and paste into a collage symbolic images filled with intention.

While on retreat in California, Connie learns that her college-age son, at home in Chicago, has severely broken his leg in a soccer accident and will undergo surgery to repair it early the next morning. Distance prevents her from getting home in time, so she decides to stay for the remainder of the retreat. In silence, she thoughtfully gathers her materials and meticulously scissors her son's image from a photograph, pastes it in the center of a piece of paper, and surrounds his likeness with pictures symbolizing courage and healing, clipped from magazines. The following day, our circle of women gathers before dawn, while in Chicago David's surgery begins. Connie places her visual prayer in the center beside the candle, and we pray in silence for David's healing and safe passage through the operation. That afternoon we learn that all is well and that he will recover completely. One year later, Connie's visual prayer graces the family's refrigerator as a reminder of the healing that continues to flow.

We make visual prayers for myriad reasons. Opportunities to create touchstones for others and for ourselves present themselves in many ways. Sometimes the crafting becomes a co-creative process.

My mother and I reconnect after months of working through painful family issues. We are inspired to make a quilt together to celebrate our renewed relationship. I select assorted fabrics in shades of purple, the color for healing. Later I gather cherished photographs and other meaningful images and transfer them to muslin, to be integrated into the pattern. We decide the design should be a crazy quilt, to reflect our complicated journey.

My mother, an artist with needle and thread, cuts the fabrics into random shapes and pieces them like a puzzle into unified form. During this collaborative process she moves to a new home, but our project continues to sew our hearts together across the miles. While she stitches, I gather ribbons, charms, and tokens from my dresser drawer: a silver moon button from a favorite dress, an ivory rose pin that belonged to my grandmother, a yellow silk pansy. I send these things and other talismans to my mother. She touches them with her special brand of quilt-making magic.

Months later she arrives for a visit, carrying a shopping bag filled with sacred cargo wrapped carefully in tissue paper. Together, with ritual and tears, we hang it in my prayer room. It is an exquisite tapestry of love. On the back of the quilt my mother made a small pocket from a fabric photo image of us as a young mother and her little girl, and placed in it her story of the quilt. The photo reminds me that I'm now older than she was when the picture was taken. This visual prayer presents me with the metaphor of how the bits and pieces of our journeys, when pieced together, become a quilt of life. The thread binding it is made of love and forgiveness.

Time has passed since I began to put these thoughts to paper. The moon will be full tonight. The afternoon breeze sends the autumn leaves pirouetting to the ground. May we be reassured, by the observation of these wonders, that we are also moving toward fulfillment and completion.

MARY JEAN RIVERA

Mary Jean Rivera identifies with Spider Woman—in the Native American understanding of "the creative force of the Universe," a person of industry, persistence, and strength. As a presentor and contract consultant, her mission is to assist individuals, schools, businesses, and churches educate their members towards effective participation, for the well-being and unity of society. Mary has a B.A. in Sociology and an M.A. in Educational Administration and Curriculum. She has worked in education for over thirty years, as a teacher and an elementary school prinicipal. Her Web site is www.teleport.com/~mrivera.

My Grandmother Told Me This

"Keep your women friends," she said. "You will need them."

My grandmother didn't really tell me very many things that directly. But she certainly did say that, and she was very right. I think I knew, before I married, that my husband wouldn't be able to meet *all* of my needs, especially my need to share some of the more humdrum details of life. Even before we were married, he wasn't much interested in reflecting on relationships, other than ours. Oh, we enjoyed watching a sunset on the beach together, all right. And he and I never seemed to run out of things to talk about. We still don't, after thirty-three years of marriage.

But there were times that we didn't talk at all. Sometimes yelling was preferable to the silences, and led to some clarification of understanding. The children would get upset when we yelled. I tried to tell them that it was only very loud talking. I have since learned that your children cannot be your friends when you are dealing with these adult problems. Only women friends understand how these situations are, without you having to explain the details, because they live out the same scenarios. Grandma was right.

We think we are subject to rapid changes in our lives today, but we have nothing on my grandmother. She was born in the 1890s, and lived to be ninety-three. She came to California as a bride, on a cross-country train; back home in Indiana she had ridden in wagons. The first years of her marriage to a civil engineer were spent out in the desert mining country, camping virtually full time. She learned to drive when cars became available. By the time I knew her, in her sixties, she was known for her "lead foot." She would drive out to our house to visit, when my own mother hesitated to go more than a few miles from home. I remember how she came every day for a week after my brother was born, to help out. She did the household work, and I still remember how she "helped" me take a bath, when I had been doing it on my own for years. It was my grandmother who took me to the beauty parlor for the first time, when I was ten or eleven. She had my hair cut and styled, and the beautician tried to teach me how to care for it. I know this trip came from the goodness of my grandmother's heart, but it offended my mother, who had neither money nor time for such "foolishness." I appreciated this attention, this teaching of things I wanted to know, things that seemed pretty practical, if not to my mother.

We had great family reunions at every major holiday, when all the aunts and uncles and cousins gathered at her house, everyone bringing food along with the babies. Children were shooed from the kitchen, but the talk and laughter of women drifted out to us, along with the banging of pots and pans and the clink of dishes in the sink.

Her large dining-room table was let out to its full length, and card tables were set up in corners for the children's seating. Everyone had china plates, real silverware, and linen napkins at these feasts. Everyone talked, uncles argued, children grew restive and over-tired, and finally we all drifted away to our homes. Grandma hugged and kissed everyone good-bye at the doorstep. It must have been a lot of work for her, but she never complained of it.

I know she went to church faithfully on Sundays, and worked on church suppers and other committees. She was never preachy, but her faith in God supported her and all of us with her. She was so confident of the Next Life, that I think she lived every moment of this life without remorse or regret. She faced the death of my father with strength, visiting or calling often during his last illness, and participating with the family regarding decisions we had to make about this care. Though tearful, she was sensible and resigned about what needed to be done.

I visited Grandmother several times during my engagement. She understood and sympathized about situations then, shared with me about our common relatives. When I married, she came to the wedding, in her first plane ride at age seventy-five. And for my wedding gift, she gave me a pair of yellow baby-doll pajamas!

"Keep your women friends. You will need them." She must have turned to her friends many times in her life, during good times and bad. They lived nearby. Together they put on spaghetti dinners and held rummage sales to help pay the church debt, took food to the bereaved and the sick, and had card parties. Surely these events were full of talk, that talk of women whose daily lives were filled with children and laundry and cooking, as mine came to be also. But for my grandmother and her friends, who outlived their husbands by as much as thirty years, there would also have been the comfort that came from sharing parallel lives, facing illnesses, death, tragedies, and old age, laced with laughter and joy in the foibles and achievements of family and self.

I didn't realize how much I needed my women friends while my children were growing up, but then, those friendships were mostly built on our children's activities, rather than on true personal commonalities. When the children's lives ceased to run parallel lines, the "friendships" sort of vanished. Upon reflection, I discovered in my internal program this motto: "Choose your friends; don't let them choose you." This advice was given to me by a trusted teacher—it was advice I tried to live by, and it did untold damage. I think my attitude of judgment was plastered on my forehead for all to see! No wonder I had no close friends then. At fifty-five, I feel that I have a web of women friends, each of whom I prize highly. I think it is important to have friends of all ages. I see some of them frequently, some of them no more than once a year. Every one of them is a special gift.

The first step for me in gaining friends was in recognizing the disservice my motto was doing me. For potential friends are all around, and not one of them is perfect. If I waited for perfect people to be my chosen friends, there would be none at all! Each person I meet has something to offer—a piece of knowledge, a skill, a special gift of laughter, a gentle touch, or a capacity for kindness. And some of them just need me to give what I can, without return, except the return that comes from giving itself. Giving and receiving turn out to be the same thing, two sides of the same event. Perhaps one of the blessings of later life is knowing who you are, and if you have accepted that, then you are ready to be a friend and to have friends. Friendship can come at any age, but it matures in time.

My group of friends shows a range of ages, interests, and character traits. Some are married, some are not, and some are divorced. Some are in delicate health and pursue few interests, as they have little strength or stamina. Others have full-time jobs and outside interests as well, in arts and crafts, or martial arts, or social-service activities. Some read a lot or attend shows or travel, and others never do such things. But without exception, each is working on her own "soul development," her purpose for this life. Each has questions about the meaning of life, and together we are searching for answers. Our focus on developing spirituality is our only common thread. Each of us seems to have "a piece of the wisdom," and no one has it all.

So, once a year, we gather to compare notes, and to lay out our pieces of the jigsaw puzzle of life, to see where it is leading us. And knowing that we will always meet again gives me "wings" to lift my spirit and carry me throughout the year.

Our group is called "Wings," and it meets annually for a retreat, which we plan for ourselves. One member acts as treasurer—she keeps the books, commits us to our retreat site each year, and hires a cook to free us from those tasks. Another member acts as a coordinator, calling the initial planning meeting sometime in late summer or early fall. We settle on a theme or main idea, sometimes drawing it from a book, sometimes developing the idea from scratch. The planning committee is a voluntary involvement—sooner or later someone works up the brochure, does the mailing or phone calling, and establishes the schedule for the weekend. New women friends are invited every year, to give us new life, and to add to our circle. Altogether, twenty-five to thirty women attend each year, but it's never exactly the same group. "Wings" meets annually on Superbowl weekend, in antithesis to that male bonding experience, from dinnertime Friday through noon on Sunday.

Each retreat is unique. Every step of our planning is covered in prayer, although the members belong to several denominations, or none at all. A typical weekend has an opening session on Friday evening, during which the housekeeping rules and the theme are set out. The rest of the evening is given to playing games and visiting, with lots of laughter. We remember the past year by sharing our memories, and we come to know more about our new attendees.

Saturday includes up to four sessions or presentations; each is usually followed by a small group discussion and time for journaling or reflection, although there are many variations on this plan. Sandwiched among the scheduled activities are exercise breaks, walks in the woods, and private talks in corners. Lastly, on Saturday night, there is always a "fire circle." Everyone brings all her half-used candles, and we light them all, seating ourselves in a loose single circle around the "fire." Personal sharing progresses as we pass around a symbol of temporary prominence (a feather, or a special rock, for example). We share—as each is led to share and only what each wishes to share—about the retreat itself, feelings, or some other insight. As each of us speaks, the others maintain respectful silence.

Sunday, after breakfast, our final session and closing prayers are followed by a flurry of leave-taking.

The environment of a retreat weekend is very important. It must allow both privacy and opportunity for conversation, and must have a space large enough for the entire group to sit facing the center. This circular seating arrangement includes everyone as equals, and avoids any position of dominance. Objects or pictures that speak to the theme provide a place to rest the eyes and focus the thoughts. Everyone gets a comfortable sleeping area with a name tag on the door, and a welcoming package giving the agenda and needed information in writing. Roommates are assigned with great care, for compatibility and opportunity for growth. We always include a memento, a small object to keep. "Heartstones"—rocks inscribed with a word such as "courage" or "delight"—have been our favorites, but there are many other possibilities. These are given out by "chance," as we are led by the Spirit after praying over them.

Our topics have included the exploration of dreams, play, passages in life, the "dance of intimacy," the interplay of personalities, personal stories, healing of memories, and the wisdom of women of other times. We avoided the topic of death until the year so many of us experienced the deaths of relatives and friends that the topic presented itself at the retreat, and could not be avoided any longer. We had a moving candlelight memorial service in the woods, "letting go" of those who have now gone before us. We performed skits, laughing till our sides ached. We planned our retreat using a consensus process involving those who came to the planning sessions. Our group has included teachers, computer consultants, data-entry personnel, social-service workers, a chaplain, homemakers, nurses, singers, and dancers. We make use of all our available talent, and even occasionally hire a massage therapist for the retreat. (We design our own presentations and scripts, but professional retreat masters are available to groups for a fee.)

This group held its early retreats in homes, doing all of its own chores, to keep costs as low as possible. But the planning members have come to see the greater value of being freed for a few days to indulge in activities, rituals, conversation, and reflection. The core group is able to fund a few "scholarships" so that others may be assisted. The cost of using a local, church-sponsored retreat facility is still nominal. The facility design is perfect, with many bedrooms and bathrooms, a very large living-room area, and a fully staffed kitchen, all in a beautiful setting surrounded by trees.

Over the years we have seen members come and go, but no one escapes unchanged. Life is about change. Some have given up smoking, alcohol, or other addictions. Others have turned to new directions in their work lives, encouraged or inspired by their retreat experiences. Acceptance by this group has provided to all who come a safe opportunity to explore creative gifts in drama and humor. Some have shared their personal stories at retreat for the first time in their lives.

"I love it! I love the sharing of wisdom! It really helps me appreciate the wisdom of other women." (SC)

"I haven't been able to come every year. What is important is that we have a history together, as we know as we grow older this is a group we can be with. Up until last year all the women were involved in cleaning up old "stuff" in their lives, but there is less of that now. That shows growth. We made a quilt together one year. Whenever it appears, it's a great sign of who we are." (MDS)

There is a sense of accountability from year to year, an acceptance of our responsibility to stretch and grow, and to bring those feats back for us to celebrate together. We have witnessed the personal growth of women who sat silently withdrawn in the beginning—growth as shown through presentations, sharing times, and voluntary involvement in planning experiences for others in following years. What powerful ingredients in life are love and the experience of success.

Mutual support extends beyond the weekend of the retreat. One member undergoing kidney dialysis received the offer of a donated kidney from two others! Later that year, we held a healing ceremony a week before the surgery for the donor and the recipient. We wrapped them in the quilt we had made. Earlier, the recipient and a group also met to plan the possible funeral. The transplant was a great success, with the joy multiplied by at least twenty-five! Other life events similarly call forth a prayerful response.

My grandmother's friends kept their togetherness in ways that were appropriate to their times. My friends and I stay together in this way, not bound by a particular neighborhood, church affiliation, or work. For the most part, our husbands do not even know each other, and generally, we do not socialize a great deal outside of retreat planning sessions and retreat weekends. Once we all took an early-morning walk in the mall together. We visit by phone and e-mail mostly, as we are each busy throughout the year in our separate lives with spouses, children, and work commitments. There are some longtime friendships within the group, but they do not overshadow or hinder the retreat experiences.

The bonds among us are indeed powerful, providing an invisible safety net, a place of belonging in the spirit. No one knows the future, but I look to it with confidence that this group will continue to meet. As we age, we will reflect on our lives, and grow together, toward perfect wholeness, "holiness." There is a saying that "we are not humans having a spiritual experience, but spiritual beings having a human experience." Our spirituality is cloaked, hidden in this human form that is the instrument of our learning. Genuine friendships do give us "wings," so that our spirits can soar.

PAT SAMPLES

Pat Samples is a transformational educator and writer.
She is the editor of The PHOENIX, *a Minnesota-based*
newspaper that focuses on personal growth, and she has published
widely on health, aging, learning, and human behavior.
Her five books include Daily Comforts for Caregivers *and*
Self-Care for Caregivers: A Twelve Step Approach. *Samples gives*
talks, classes, and workshops on caregiving, conscious aging,
and other personal development topics. She has a son
who makes her smile and a canary that reminds
her to sing. Her essay is reprinted from
The PHOENIX, *with permission.*

Ulτimaτe Celebraτions

We were pallbearers, the ten of us. Terry had planned it that way—not that she would die so young, but that we, her women's group, would bear her to her grave. Twelve years ago, that time came upon us suddenly, without warning.

Only a few months earlier, we had gathered for our monthly meeting, and—at Terry's invitation—we each planned our own funeral. At that time, none of us was ill or particularly concerned about imminent death; we were women lovingly tending to one another's lives, who were also willing to anticipate and prepare together for our deaths. A dozen years later, when most of us had passed fifty, and one of us had been diagnosed with a terminal illness, we would meet again to revisit our funeral plans with a greater sense of urgency. This first time, however, borne by the early tides of women's liberation, I think we did the funeral planning as much to claim self-direction in our lives and to clarify what was important to us as to make end-of-life plans.

Both times, the experience brought us closer to one another and to the centers of our own souls.

The first time, Terry suggested the activity. Our group had been meeting for eight years by then; our meetings began when a close friend and I asked women we knew if they would like to meet regularly for personal support. (The group, still in existence today after twenty years, has changed some in membership over time, but even those no longer participating are treated as extended family.) By the time Terry proposed the planning, we had become quite a close group. We had lovingly tended to one another through troubled marriages, child-rearing challenges, and schooling and career evolutions, as we emerged along with the women's movement into our individual and collective sense of power and worth.

Planning our funerals together was another way to tend to one another's lives. While most of us were still in our thirties and forties, we had all by then had some involvement in preparing the funeral of a family member or friend, with nothing to guide us. We knew that it would be helpful, when we died, to leave behind something that revealed our preferences. But even more important, it would be enlightening in the present to know what special things most mattered to each person in the group as she thought about the end of her life.

Terry provided each of us with a set of questions to consider, and I remember being both uneasy and intrigued as I set out to answer them and the other questions that came to my mind. Who could I imagine being in attendance and willing and able to give readings, make comments, or otherwise participate? Would my then-husband, so much older than I, still be alive? Would my son have good things to say about me? Would my family, who had abandoned me when I married a black man "outside the church," even come? How would my friends feel the loss? What would comfort them? How would I want them to remember my accomplishments? What music would best reveal my heart and soul, and open theirs? Would I want my brother, a traditional priest, to officiate (as he had at other family funerals), or would I prefer that the radical pastor of my own church, whose message better reflects my current way of living, conduct the funeral?

As each of us sifted through such questions and revealed our own preferences at that meeting, Terry's were the most striking—perhaps because she had given the subject the most thought, or perhaps because she had a love and flair for designing meaningful ritual. What particularly touched us all was when she declared that we, the members of her women's group, were to be her pallbearers.

Just a few months later, full-hearted Terry, with her long dark hair and bangs, and her full-sized body always draped in loose, earthy dresses, died suddenly in her sleep. Her warm wisdom and laughter had mothered us all, and now we were to bury her. Filled with grief, we took to heart the wishes she had shared with us, and added to them what we knew would please her and also express what she meant to us. Her husband, deep in shock, was happy to turn the planning over to us and a couple of her other friends, Catholic nuns who shared Terry's bent for womanly rituals.

Terry's funeral was to be a reflection of her life, and as such, it would be a celebration of creativity and spirituality. Because she had many friends, it would also be a celebration of friendship and community. And we all knew that she liked ritual, symbols, and ceremony.

As we gathered for the planning, it was easy to imagine her smiling on us, knowing she was creating even now what she most loved—a gathering of caring, creative women preparing to express their joys and sorrows together in communal celebration.

A ribbon—green, for hope—was unrolled at the wake and passed from person to person in the crowded funeral-home parlor. Each person receiving the roll was invited to tell a story or to make comments about Terry's life. Her humor, mothering, leadership, friendship, creativity, compassion, and defiance of staid and oppressive systems were all cited and celebrated. The green ribbon became a river flowing among and between us, creating a common bed for our tears and ripples for our joy. When all was said and sung, scissors were passed, and we each left carrying the piece of ribbon we had clutched.

Each of us from the group remembers a few things from the funeral that have stayed in our souls. I remember the processional, led by friends carrying large pastel banners bearing symbols and words representing values that mattered to Terry: peace and love and justice. The music was a mix of the tender and the triumphant, beginning with "On Eagles' Wings"—*I will raise you up on eagles' wings, bear you on the breath of dawn, make you to shine like the sun, and hold you in the palm of My hand.*

Gayle, who was a close friend to Terry, remembers Terry's teenage daughter, Katie, getting up to thank her mother for the curled-up-on-the-bed times they had shared, and their sitting on the beach together comparing "hunks" passing by (which made us all laugh). Diane remembers reading aloud a letter she had written to Terry, in which she said how much she would miss her friend, and asked, "How's it going where you are? Did you find a women's group? I'll just bet you're organizing one right now." Tears flowed, but at the end, we followed Terry's coffin up the church aisle singing a song of joy, as Terry would have wanted: *I am not dying. I am dancing, dancing along in the madness—there is no sadness, only a song in my soul.*

What each of us remembers most markedly was being among Terry's pallbearers. I felt so honored. I walked tall, with pride in being a woman and in being her friend. The coffin was very heavy, even for ten of us; Terry was robust not only in spirit but also in size, and Gayle, in her usual bold-humor fashion, whispered an aside that we should have made her go on a diet years ago. The laughter and tears together were almost too much to bear. After the graveyard service, people stayed to talk, to remember, to stay tied to one another a little longer. Terry had given us a day in which to cherish her life and our own, together.

Not long ago, some of us gathered again to think anew about what would be important to us at the ends of our lives. Death seemed more imminent this time, the planning more necessary, because at least one of us is at high risk for leaving before long, and we are all in the second halves of our lives. Although I am no longer a regular member of this women's group, there are still many ties that bind, and I was glad they wanted me to be there.

The circumstances that prompted our gathering this time, plus our memories of Terry's sudden death, prompted a heightened attentiveness as we listened to each person's requests. This was a time of sacred telling and listening.

Margaret, a woman outspoken on justice for children and the powerless, was heading to remote regions in Africa to volunteer for a few months. She was unsure about her safety there, and had written her funeral plans in detail. They included a favorite reading on "living out loud." She also had put a few precious belongings in a little box—sand from every beach she had loved, rings, and other mementos with meaning for her—to be given to specific people when she dies. Margaret said she could leave the country feeling more secure now, knowing that, if she didn't return alive, her intentions had been put in the care of the group.

Marin, a librarian and an artist who loves traditions and old furniture, said she wants the standard Lutheran funeral, with lunch afterward provided by the altar guild. She has no preferences regarding liturgy or music, she said; it would all be handled by the appropriate people at church. But she had made a list of treasured antiques and other belongings, carefully designating the recipient for each.

By contrast, with her ever-present grin, Rita said she wants a church service, but not the traditional Catholic Mass she once valued. More importantly, she wants a get-together on her lawn, potluck as I recall, where everyone can have a good time and be in nature, near her gardens.

Ever-sociable Donna, who laughs often as she tells of her seemingly constant losses to fate and circumstance, said there was nothing for her to decide. Everything would be done according to Jewish tradition. She seemed surprised by that realization, but content with it.

As we took turns, pouring out our final preferences into the circular receiving vessel formed by the reverent presence of faithful and loving friends, each of us reflected the most essential truths of her life. Margaret has always "lived out loud"—she knows and cherishes that about herself, and so do we. Rita has a fondness for growing things, and she never wants people to fuss over her. Donna is most at home in her Jewish origins, and she has often looked to others to decide for her. As in life, so in death.

Each woman's plans struck me as so simple. Decades of momentous and minute life events, relationships, and belongings would be saluted briefly with a few mementos and rituals. Our lives would be over. How wonderful, then, that in this gathering we were able to ask, and to trust, that this group would remember what mattered to us.

I was one of the last to speak, and although I asked to have a final service in my current church with its wonderful musicians, I was feeling such contentment and sweet-sad awe over what we were doing together that I felt no pressing need for more specific instructions. The presence of loving and faithful friends who cared about me, in my living and in my dying, seemed sufficient. My heart was full, my spirit satisfied.

DEBORAH STRAW

*Deborah Straw is a writer, editor and teacher who lives
in Burlington, Vermont, and spends several months each year in
Key West, Florida. Straw writes and publishes essays, short stories,
book reviews, poems, and articles. She also teaches writing and
literature courses at the Community College of Vermont and
is the Writing Assessment Mentor at the Burlington campus.
Her book,* Natural Wonders of the Florida Keys, *was
recently published. Her second book,* Why Is Cancer
Killing Our Pets?: How You Can Protect and
Treat Your Animal Companion,
will be published this fall.

a Writer's Gift

It happened again today. A student with stars in her eyes stopped me and told me how much I had given her. No, the "stars in the eyes" line is not arrogance. I see the eyes twinkle, and I remember the feeling. I've had these feelings, too. I was fortunate enough to have had a wise woman mentor, who changed my world just when I needed her to do so.

May Sarton was the author of more than fifty books, including *Kinds of Love* and *Journal of a Solitude*. She was the most passionate, giving friend and teacher I have ever known, giving me her permission (to give myself permission) to write poems and short stories, something I had not dared to do until I met her. She also urged me to spend more time writing and less time teaching. She had discovered that writing and teaching take the same psychic energy, and that writers cannot afford to give away too much of their primary energy.

Through her loving, unwavering example, I learned the importance and power of mentoring other women.

In my thirties, I had come to Sarton's table with a moderate amount of confidence. My parents had always been proud of me, had encouraged me through my college years and even through my '60s radical activities against the Vietnam War. But I had no role models of professional women artists, and an artist is what I wanted to be. May Sarton was my favorite author. So from somewhere deep inside I grabbed the courage to attempt to meet her. When the author, thirty-six years my senior, was scheduled to come to our town for a book signing, I invited her for dinner at our house, and she accepted.

May came, we ate a gourmet dinner, drank Scotch, and hit it off. Thus began our intense relationship. After that first meeting, we met every two or three months. Each time, she was an inspiring conversationalist, and she was enthusiastic about my writing endeavors. We began with niceties (weather talk, discussion about birds or our cats) and a cup of tea, but almost right away, she wanted to know what I was writing. She uttered a hearty "Bravo!" when I took a new risk. During those years of high excitement, she encouraged me to experiment. I tried many genres—poetry, personal essay, short fiction. She recommended and loaned to me books by authors, particularly women authors, she considered fine or unusual—Virginia Woolf, Ruth Pitter, Hilda Doolittle. May also gave me her own writing, even a few of the rare, out-of-print volumes.

We also discussed her projects—her frustrations, deadlines, and recent reviews, both praising and damning. She talked of relationships, past and present, with editors, agents, readers, and critics, and she related stories of her early mentors, Virginia Woolf and Belgian poet Jean Dominique—thrilling names from a glorious past literary world.

May consistently offered encouragement, ideas about markets, and feedback on a title or topic. When she read something of mine, she was cautiously positive and firmly critical. She told me one or two things she liked very much—a word here, an image there—and one or two things she thought needed work. It was hard to hear her criticism, but I knew it was good for me. Between our visits, when she wasn't immersed in a manuscript, May wrote me wonderful letters. Like her books, they were graciously worded, about nature, friends, books, and, of course, ideas. From the night of that first dinner at our home, there was no turning back. I knew she was giving me a wonderful gift.

Through Sarton's example, I became more able to develop and share my talents by daring to write about what matters. May wrote unflinchingly about cancer; about infidelity; about depression; about hatred and prejudice; about friends and animals dying; about feeling suicidal. Through many of her poems and, especially, her journal entries, she made me realize that these were profound, legitimate topics about which to write, and that there was an audience for them. She came out of the closet in her novel *Mrs. Stevens Hears the Mermaids Singing* when it was unfashionable to do so, and she suffered professional repercussions, but she did it. She taught me that daily life and relationships are what really matter in this life; the way we lead our lives and treat others influences our mental and physical health.

I discovered, as had Sarton, that writing down my thoughts and shaping and revising them into some cogent form ordered my world. I realized what was important, and what I needed to focus on. I discovered what I felt and thought about a number of issues that prior to knowing Sarton I might not even have recognized as pressing in my life. Instead of writing solely about subjects I had little interest in, offered up by editors, I began to write about women's friendships and women's relationships to their homes, to mentors, to the natural world, and to domestic animals. I've discovered passionate and polished writing generally can find a home.

As a result of knowing May Sarton, I took steps to ensure that I kept writing. Ten years ago, I started a writers' group of published women writers; our biweekly Sunday evening meetings have become a highlight of my life. They provide an informal deadline and a discipline I haven't always had. The solitude of the writing life is one of the reasons I continue to teach. I like teaching, and I believe in helping beginning writers, many of whom have had no role model for an academic or professional life.

Today, a student—I'll call her Kate—needed to be given permission, as I had those twelve years ago. Kate has nearly completed a narrative essay about a small, incestuous town in northern Vermont. She said, "Oh, I couldn't send that out. Some readers would think I was snobby." "So what?" I asked. I told her you have to be true to your vision of the world. Readers who can relate will find you and other readers will find writers whose vision of life they share. In the best of all worlds, readers who differ from the writer's world vision or social class but love her words will also read her. Kate is bursting at the seams to tell her life's stories, as I have been on many occasions. Both of us needed a wiser woman to encourage us to begin.

Without Sarton's influence and power, I could not have so encouraged Kate's talent or so understood her situation. Sarton not only urged me to write more, she convinced me to believe in my own power, in my own vision of the world. I believe that most of us have great creative potential, but we need to be coaxed out of our shells to share these talents.

Kate is but one writer whose self-belief and talents I have helped rekindle. These women students and I keep finding each other. They all love language, have a deeply creative source which may have been squelched, and come to love Sarton's and other women writers' works.

Terry, twenty, came into class with a weak vocabulary and unfocused ideas. Now she is writing tight and mature essays about the importance of her elderly dog and art in her daily life, and has decided to apply to become an art therapist; she has just the right heart and personality to do so.

Sally began putting her ninety-year life on paper in a memoir-writing group at an adult day care center. Drawing on a rich life of travel, marriages, children, and grandchildren, she began to get up in the middle of the night to jot down her thoughts. She noticed every bird and the way moonlight cast shadows on her apartment walls. And she lived to see her work, her life, published.

I continue to pass along the gift.

HOPE SWANN

*Describing herself as a Pilgrim, Wife, Mother, Grandmother,
Green Witch, Neophyte Crone, Mostly Vegetarian,
Buddheo-Christian-Neopagan-Ecofeminist, and Creatrix of
whimsy, mayhem, ritual, and laughter, Hope Swann is grateful
for the teachers and the teachings she has encountered during travel
on five continents and living in seven U.S. states and Mexico.
She has learned that it doesn't matter how many workshops you
attend or crystals you wear. What matters is being compassionate
with yourself and all beings, paying attention and setting
intention, and expressing gratitude. Her store in Charlotte,
North Carolina, is called The Bag Lady.*

how I Became a Bag Lady

Five years ago, when I was forty-eight, my uncle left me a small inheritance that I was slowly spending without much to show for it, except an ever-decreasing balance on my bank statement. I knew that if I didn't do something with the remaining money, it would soon be gone, and I would be disgusted with myself. But I was also panic-stricken at the thought of losing my nest egg by investing it foolishly. What if: I took a risk . . . lost the money . . . my husband died . . . and I had nothing . . . What if . . . What if . . . ?

I had always dreamed of owning a woman's bookshop with, of course, wonderful books, but also wonderful, empowering Womanstuff, as well. However, in these days of bookstore chains and e-commerce, even I recognized this as fantasy. So what else was there that I wanted to do?

My husband's father and his wife ran a small shop in Florida specializing in handmade canvas tote bags. Their business had been quite successful, and they had offered to help me get started in the canvas-bag business if that was something I might be interested in doing. Although the bags were lovely, I just wasn't all that excited about making and selling them. Still, their success made it sound do-able and not too risky. I began to toy with the idea of having a bag shop. Perhaps a shop in which I made the bags and carried other things of interest to women that might go into the bags . . . like maybe . . . even . . . books! Instead of having a bookshop with wonderful stuff, maybe I could have a wonderful-stuff shop with books . . . and . . . bags.

For several months, permutations of this basic idea percolated in my head. I vacillated wildly between a giddy euphoria (in which I planned entire emporiums of fabulous goodies for women) and the angst of the harsh reality outlined by my ever-present Inner Critic (in which I was reminded in no uncertain terms that the sum of my retail experience consisted of four short-term basic cashier's jobs, and that I was certain to end up broke and on the street).

During these down times, my husband reminded me that not only was he steadily employed and would do his best to keep me from becoming a streetwalker, but that if I did go "belly-up" and become a bag lady, I would certainly be a quite fashionable one, with sturdy, functional, and water-resistant canvas tote bags. And so it was that I decided should I ever actually do this insane thing, I would call my shop "The Bag Lady: Provisions for the Wild Woman."

Months passed and the internal debate escalated. "The Bag Lady" became clearer and clearer in my mind. Charlotte, North Carolina, a Bible-Belt beachhead, definitely needed a place with resources for women. The Bag Lady wouldn't be a feminist store, or a

New Age store, or a lesbian store, but a place for women of all ages, sizes, shapes, and skin colors; religious, sexual and political preferences; economic status and astrological signs! It would be a place where a wealthy Baptist matron (whose idea of a Women's Circle was a Junior League meeting) and a green-haired Gen-Xer with a multitude of pierced parts might each find something to enrich her life and nourish her spirit. The Bag Lady would be a place where a woman could walk in and find a book that might change her life . . . or maybe just buy bubble bath to celebrate making it through another day. It would be a place where she could come to find good conversation, a belly laugh, or a Kleenex for her tears.

As The Bag Lady became clearer, the Critic became louder. Did this town (or anyplace else) need yet another retail establishment? Did I really want to further the plague of consumerism? Were the things I would offer just be a distraction from the inner work that truly empowers and supports women? And further, was I just plain crazy? Retail is risky business. Most shops fail within the first three years. I knew next to nothing about what I was getting into. What made me think I should or could do this? Maybe I was just . . . hormonal . . . ARGHHHH!

Daily, I inched closer to the proverbial "poop-or-get-off-the-pot" point. I made lists. I tore up lists. I designed floor spaces on graph paper. I tore them up. I argued with myself endlessly. Surely it would be better to attempt this dream and fail, than not to do it and know I hadn't even tried. The Critic replied that this was all quite noble, but we were talking about money here, and the potential absence of same, and why didn't I just put it in a good mutual fund? (The Critic at this point sounded a good bit like my uncle from whom the money had come . . .)

One day in the midst of all this turmoil, I pulled out a book that I had purchased some months before—*Meeting the Madwoman: Empowering the Feminine Spirit*, by Linda Schierse Leonard. I had started reading it once before, but just couldn't get into it. Guiltily, I picked it up now, thinking that since I had spent the money on it, I really should give it a second shot before tossing it into the "take to the library" box.

The book fell open in my hand to chapter six, which was titled "The Bag Lady." *Uh-oh.*

I read that "Beneath the surface . . . many women are secretly afraid that they would crumble if they were completely on their own. Their worst fantasy imaginable is that they wouldn't be able to take care of themselves, materially or emotionally. They are afraid they might deteriorate, stop coping, let everything go, and end up poor and homeless. Their fantasies reflect a fear of 'losing it,' a fear that is very real in a culture that measures success by the quantity of one's possessions, and especially one that works against the development of a strong, feminine spirit." This all sounded painfully familiar.

I read that "Bag Lady fears often come up when a woman is about to make an important change in her life. . . ." I read that "Fear of becoming the Bag Lady often keeps a woman from taking the risks necessary to having a creative and spiritual life. . . ."

And of course I read much, much more. Including an example of a woman confronting The Bag Lady archetype, who, despite her fears, left her successful career to do what she really loved rather than what she felt (or others said) she should be doing. To support herself she worked in a shop making canvas tote bags. *Uh-oh.*

OK. So even I can "get" a message from the Universe when it's written in flashing neon and personally addressed to me. Even I could see that Bag Lady peering over my shoulder as I looked in the mirror, daring me to—finally—step out of my fears and into Myself.

So I told my husband that I would call his father to talk to him about a bag shop. He wisely responded, "When?" I testily replied, "Saturday." Knowing me very well, he replied, "When on Saturday?" "Noon, damnit."

On Saturday at noon, I sat frozen by the phone. My husband casually reminded me of the time. "I'm not ready!" I snapped in reply, just as the phone rang. It was his father, who apologized and said he had meant to dial my husband's sister, not me, but had inadvertently hit the wrong auto-dial button. *Uh-oh.* "No," I sighed, "it was me you were supposed to call."

On March 1, 1995, "The Bag Lady: Provisions for the Wild Woman" opened in Charlotte, North Carolina, full of "Wonderful, Whimsical, Womanstuff." With the mission to "Nurture, Celebrate and Empower Women," her walls were filled with journals and candles and tarot cards; women's art and greeting cards; balms and tonics for body and soul; adornments and talismans; spiritual travel guides; meditation cushions; tools for creativity; lotions and potions; books, gifts, and oh, yeah, bags.

Within a few months of opening, however, it became apparent that some interesting shifts were occurring. The bags, intended to be the "bread and butter" of the shop, weren't selling. The "other stuff," the things I loved and had wanted to carry all along, were going like wild-fire! So I began to phase out the bags. And to trust my own intuition.

But if there were to be no bags, I realized, then "The Bag Lady" part of my name wouldn't make any sense. Further, I had begun to wonder about the wisdom of aligning my business (and myself) with an image long associated with women's dysfunction, powerlessness, and poverty. So I began to redefine "The Bag Lady"—my business, the archetype I feared, and myself—as "A strong, resourceful woman who travels lightly and carries with her what she needs. A woman who isn't afraid to take risks, who relies on her inner strengths (intuition, intention, wit, creativity, and compassion) to travel within herself and out into the world. She is a maiden, a mother, and finally, a crone. She is a survivor. She has savvy, pizzazz, chutzpah, elan, aplomb, style, soul, power, heart . . . she is a Wild Woman."

Once I put her on paper, she began to manifest in my life, her negative power transformed. By listening to myself, and facing, embracing, and transforming The Bag Lady archetype, she became my ally.

Through her, I faced many of the fears of The Bag Lady: aging, self-worth, and body image issues; fears of failure . . . and of success; fears of powerlessness, and fears of what will happen when I am finally able to assume my own power as a crone. I have looked her in the face, and though she still frightens me at times, I can laugh with her at others. She and I spiral into them together, and I return with new ways of looking at myself, of further redefining myself. As I am growing stronger, I am becoming more capable of taking risks, and I am becoming my own advocate. I am claiming the power of The Bag Lady, on my own terms, according to my own definition.

By following my dream and opening my gift and bookshop for women, I paradoxically know that if it failed tomorrow, not only would I survive, but I will have grown from the experience. Most importantly, in addition to facing these fears, I have discovered my "bag" contains those Bag Lady tools I had listed: intuition, intention, wit, creativity, and compassion. And there are many more tools I am discovering every day: the tools that will enable me to face the other real and imagined fears I will surely encounter as I continue along the Path of the Crone. By creating this shift within myself, as I enter my Crone Passage, I have hopefully helped open the way for other women to do the same.

"The Bag Lady: Provisions for the Wild Woman" prospers. The wild women of Charlotte, North Carolina, have embraced her. We moved from our original small space to another one almost double in size. My original staff of one (me!) has grown to include a full-time staff of five, including a Vice Goddess (one of her perks is that she is allowed to interpret that anyway she wishes), a Supreme Bodacious Bagette, and two Bagettes. Although we have a hierarchical structure, we meet in circle and sisterhood. The Bag Lady supports the Battered Women's Shelter in a variety of ways. She sponsors bookclubs and co-sponsors a monthly series of women's dialogues in the community. She mentored the opening of a similar shop in Columbus, Ohio. She continues to look for ways to develop and expand her outreach. The Bag Lady, redefined, is alive and well. Me, too.

HELEN VANDERVORT

Helen Vandervort's Crone credentials include mother, grandmother, wife, small business owner, caregiver for her ninety-six-year-old mother, and holder of an M.A. degree in Communications, earned when she was fifty years old. A Certified Fund Raising Executive, she has had over thirty years' experience in public relations, development, administration, and fundraising counseling. An active community volunteer, skier, and hiker, Helen is now concentrating on her writing.

No More Waiting

Wait your turn. Wait until you grow up. Wait until next year. While we hold back expectantly for whatever is desired, we keep ourselves busy in an effort to make the time go more quickly, or to prepare for those unrealized desires—the promotion, the vacation, the baby, the cure. One wait is more difficult to understand: "Just wait until you get old!" That's a favorite phrase of my mother, who lives with us. She is ninety-six years old and amazingly alert, although her body is beginning to betray her. The meaning of the phrase eludes me. Perhaps if she added, "Then you'll understand," or some other qualifier, I'd "get it." Of course, I could *ask* her what "Just wait until you get old" means, but that might spoil discovering the meaning on my own.

My mother, whom we call Grannie, has a small crone circle she contacts every day by telephone. While she wears a Med Alert "panic" button to secure help should she need it while I'm out of the house doing my thing, she does her own medical-alert check of her "young" friends Blanche and Pearl, who are in their eighties. Each day she inquires about their health—which is not good—and urges them to think positively. She tries to get them to talk about the happy times, after they have told her of their aches and pains. They catch memories that go back fifty, sixty, seventy years. These come easily, as do the laughter and tears that go with them. Memories of dead children, grandchildren, and long-gone friends are tempered with reminiscences of Model-T Fords, dancing the Charleston, and first airplane flights.

Grannie also telephones and writes her few surviving classmates from the School of Nursing at Glendale Sanitarium in California. Young and eager in 1923, they worked twenty-four-hour shifts, were paid six cents an hour while learning to become RNs, and, out of that, had to pay tuition, buy uniforms, books, and meal tickets. They still laugh over the time one of them bobbed her hair and was threatened with expulsion, and the time my mother sent lemonade to the lab for urine analysis. They recall the movie stars who came to the sanitarium to receive gold shots for syphilis, or to be cured of drug and alcohol abuse. Grannie talks of Clara Bow, Ben Turpin, and other stars whose names have faded from her memory. It was heady stuff for the young student nurses.

But looking back is only part of their link. These women are fascinated by current events as they watch history being made on the small screen. They have strong opinions about politics, fashions, and sports. Most are predictable: politicians are immoral and corrupt; fashions are no longer pretty, nor ladylike; athletes are paid too much. But they do care about the world outside their small domains.

These women—old only because their bodies no longer let them do the things they love—aren't aware they have a "crone circle." If anyone referred to them as crones, they would be highly insulted, as they don't know the true meaning of the word. They would think people were referring to sagging faces, thinning hair, backs humped with osteoporosis, and body parts that do untidy things. Yet, these women are the embodiment of wisdom, givers of life despite arthritic hands and dim eyes. They are master healers and teachers, setting moral codes for their children and passing down family lore.

Barbara G. Walker, author of *The Crone: Woman of Age, Wisdom, and Power*, says, "The Old Woman, who acknowledges no master, may be our best guide in this long, dark, labyrinthine spiritual journey." She points out that women have vision within this spiritual base, and may have a dark and sensual side, as well as being respected matriarchs who wear their wrinkles as badges of honor.

Today, some of us take a certain delight in the fear that women—particularly old women—have elicited throughout history. As Robert Graves wrote in his "Muse," "The reason why the hairs stand on end, the eyes water, the throat is constricted, the skin crawls and a shiver runs down the spine when one writes or reads a true poem is that a true poem is necessarily an invocation of the White Goddess, or Muse, the Mother of All Living, the ancient power of fright and lust—female spider or the queen bee whose embrace is death."

Today's crones, witches, and goddesses don't wait to work our magic. We Race for the Cure, deliver meals-on-wheels, volunteer with the Humane Society, and read to children through the SMART Program. In the United States, women represent fifty-two percent of the population and control sixty percent of the wealth. We inherit wealth from our fathers, husbands, and other family members. We also earn it, invest it, and use it where we think it has a positive impact on our communities, the nation, and the world. Yes, we still stuff envelopes and bake cookies, but more and more, we chair foundation boards, raising hundreds of thousands—nay, millions—of dollars to support hospitals, libraries, colleges, and safe houses for women and children. We write grants; we twist arms to get checks written for our favorite causes. Our magic today is intelligence, education, position in the community, and persuasion of the feminine kind, in the most positive context.

My fellow crones and I will neither wait to get old, nor wait for Godot. Crones will not wait to have our existence explained to us. We know, because we have the life experience and the will to understand the past and the present. Crones do not wait for men to make things right. We are active in local, national, and international efforts to care for the needy, the displaced, the uneducated. We use our wisdom to make a difference. We are politically active, often quietly subversive, doing whatever it takes to help the world make sense.

We are not waiting to get old. In fact, we fight the encroaching years with every trick of the female psyche, as well as with SPF-15, vitamins, exercise, and lovers. We push on, savoring each day despite the duties and trials thrust upon us. Some battle cancer, some care for aging parents or husbands. Some rear grandchildren out of love and necessity. At times, our bodies play false with us; so we get stronger glasses, wear knee braces while hiking, or deny ourselves favorite foods, but we are the lucky ones—because we do not feel old inside. We are open to the different realities of existence, using our intuition to guide us.

The notion that "old age is woman's hell" (attributed to Ninon de L'Ecclos, 1620–1705) is untrue. All we need is "attitude" as we enjoy our so-called second adulthood. A sense of humor comes in handy as we encounter the labels bestowed upon us: *senior, mature, aged*. Why not *perfected, consummate*, or *full-fledged*?

"Just wait until you're old" is not for us—we women of a certain age in this new millennium. We are too busy to wait for anything. We live each day as if it were the last. Still, we plan trips, new bedroom curtains, or a smaller dress size. We are optimistic, looking at life as a great adventure. Crones demand freedom and independence so that ". . . when one heard that Old Age was coming, one could bolt the door, answer 'Not at home,' and refuse to meet him!" (attributed to the *Kokinshu*).

Perhaps Dylan Thomas said it best:

> *Do not go gentle into that good night,*
> *Old age should burn and rave at close of day;*
> *Rage, rage against the dying of the light.*

DIANA VILAS

Diana Vilas has earned a B.A. in English Literature from Vassar College and double Masters' degrees in psychology and transpersonal counseling. Her private practice of eighteen years started with grief counseling and evolved into spiritual growth consulting. She has taught seminars on spiritual awareness and lectured to groups of psychologists. Diana is the former editor of Crone Chronicles, *and recently had an interview with Margaret Wheatley, titled "Bringing the Goddess into the Boardroom," published in the anthology* What Matters. *A dedicated scholar of science, philosophy, religion, mysticism, astrology, and mythology, she chose to experience natural menopause and has shared her insights in her book* The Initiation of Menopause: Becoming the Spiritual Adult. *Diana lives in Jackson Hole, Wyoming, with her husband, Michael.*

The Spiritual Potential of Menopause

It is no coincidence that women of the baby-boom generation are entering menopause just as humanity is poised for a quantum leap in consciousness. Change is afoot, and the synchronistic timing of these events suggests they are woven together in the fabric of destiny.

Menopause is a relatively modern phenomenon. It's only within the last hundred years that life expectancy has extended much beyond menopause. In the eighteenth and nineteenth centuries, those women who survived childbirth died of "old age" in their forties or fifties. But today women expect to live much longer. We're starting to speak of menopause as "middle age." If we're going to live half our lives after menopause, we need to reassess this milestone, to seek deeper meaning.

Menopause has always been regarded as a biological event—the end of a woman's reproductive years, and the beginning of an inevitable decline into old age. But in 1966, Robert Wilson, M.D., turned it into a medical problem when he declared in his book,

Feminine Forever, that menopause was a deficiency disease. We get old because we run out of estrogen. To stay young, and feminine, we simply replenish our dwindling hormones. As a result, hormone replacement therapy (HRT) has become the accepted medical response to menopause, generating a billion-dollar industry sustained by advertising campaigns geared to incite our fear. Television commercials suggest that women who don't take estrogen supplements are at risk of osteoporosis and heart attack, even Alzheimer's disease.

Scientific research does not substantiate these claims, although laboratory technicians who work for drug companies keep looking for evidence. Nevertheless, there is a host of unpleasant symptoms accompanying menopause, which can be alleviated by HRT. Whether we succumb to commercial propaganda or not, we all seek relief from the assault of hot flashes, sleeplessness, weight gain, loss of libido, depression, and the seeming deterioration of memory. If we view menopause as an aging disease, then it seems logical to treat the symptoms medically—drug them away. But what if there's more to menopause than meets the eye? What if there's a spiritual purpose behind this shift in body chemistry?

When I entered menopause in 1990, I decided to find out. I combined my training in psychology and counseling with intense self-examination and extensive research in physiology, physics, chemistry, metaphysics, astrology, and mythology. What I discovered is that menopause is not just a biological event. It is a spiritual milestone with the potential for transformation, transcendence, even evolution. Menopause is a Soul initiation, an opportunity to become a Spiritual Adult.

My first challenge was to understand my symptoms. All that year I kept lowering the thermostat while everyone around me buttoned up their sweaters. I hadn't had a decent night's sleep in years and I was gaining weight on a low-fat diet, despite an hour-long daily aerobics workout. I was highly emotional and volatile. I could feel energy surging through my body almost like a low-voltage current. What was really going on? I found my first clue in science.

In 1977, a Belgian scientist named Ilya Prigogine won the Nobel Prize in Chemistry for his Theory of Dissipative Structures. What intrigued me was his conclusion about transformation. He discovered that when he added energy (in the form of heat) to a chemical solution and observed the process under a microscope, the structure intensified and the pattern got stronger, until it reached a critical point when it disintegrated into chaos. Dr. Prigogine discovered not only that it takes a lot of energy to produce transformation, but that existing patterns become stronger until energy reaches a critical mass.

I began to realize that menopause was an opportunity. All the energy formerly tied up in a chemical cycle was being released into my system. The hot flash was a symptom not of deficiency, but of potential transformation. I could view menopause as the onset of old age, or I could take advantage of all that energy for spiritual growth. I had no control over the mysterious changes in my body, but I did have the power to decide their meaning. Menopause was mine to create.

I took another look at the symptoms and reframed them within the context of spiritual transformation. I began to see the hot flash as power fueling my growth, cooking up a new identity. I was waking up, becoming more conscious, so I stopped struggling with sleeplessness. Instead I put those midnight hours to use exploring the depths of my psyche. I realized the emotional volatility was a result of my subconscious mind emptying its contents into consciousness. All the wounds, the disappointments and failures, the psychic debris of the past were erupting from my depths. And my depression wasn't pathology. It was my Soul's way of cocooning me for metamorphosis, drawing me into the depths of my pain, where healing and power awaited.

Once I reframed the symptoms and saw the spiritual potential of menopause, I realized that resistance was counterproductive. Treating the physical symptoms with hormones, or the emotional ones with mood elevators, held the threat of aborting my process. My body, in its wisdom, was cooperating with my Soul, offering me the opportunity of self-realization. I didn't want to stop the hot flashes. I needed that energy for transformation. However, I realized that put me on the brink of chaos.

We've been taught to fear chaos. It is part of our human nature to organize everything. It gives us security through a false sense of control. But science is now discovering that chaos plays an important role, not only in creativity, but in evolution as well. Chaos is what Deepak Chopra calls "pure potentiality." Anything is possible. Within chaos lie many potential futures, as well as the power to create them.

By definition, chaos is "a state of utter confusion or disorder." A new science of chaos, however, has discovered a great paradox—that within chaos lies order. In the '60s, an MIT meteorologist named Edward Lorenz was attempting to conquer weather prediction. Translating data into numbers, he fed all the variables—temperature, barometric pressure, wind currents, humidity, and a host of others—into a weather-predicting formula in his computer. Each variable was assigned a coordinate on his computer screen. At first dots appeared at random, with no seeming order, but after several hours a pattern began to appear, repeating over and over like an unfolding kaleidoscope.

Self-repeating patterns of development like these are called fractals, and fractals are like snowflakes. No two are exactly alike. Each formula creates its own unique beauty. The question is, "What is it that makes reality unfold in patterns?" No one knows, but some mystical soul named it the "Strange Attractor." Rather than pushing matter into form, a mysterious magnetic force draws energy forward into patterns of exquisite beauty. Somewhere in the future lies a blueprint, a plan.

Lorenz discovered, furthermore, that life is inherently unpredictable. The first time he ran his program, he rounded his data off to six decimal points. The second time he rounded off to three, and got totally different results—different fractal, different pattern, different weather. He concluded that weather, indeed life itself, is so complex, so intricately interwoven that the slightest detail shifts the whole. Everything matters. Everything has impact. In fact, the whole is so sensitive, that the flap of a butterfly's wings on one continent can create a tornado on another!

Out of his initial work, a new science of chaos has evolved. Theorists are studying whole systems now to observe how they interact and grow. What they have discovered is that information is the energy of the universe. Systems such as society, government, business—even individual personalities—create structure in order to hold and process information. When information reaches a critical level, it overwhelms the system. The system collapses and goes into chaos. The amazing thing about systems, however, is that if we let them evolve, they will self-organize at a higher level! Within chaos lies the future pattern of a system that can handle the increased energy efficiently.

Chaos is an enormous reservoir of energy and information. Systems evolve through a continual exchange between order and chaos. Once a system has organized around a body of information, it becomes stable and begins to decline, gradually using up its energy until it runs down. This process is called entropy. But if there is a steady stream of new information, the system is revitalized and continues to evolve into a higher, more complex order.

Armed with this reassuring information, I decided to trust the process. If systems evolved through chaos, so could I. I saw menopause as a window of opportunity wherein my body offered up its energy reserves. If I resisted, I'd lose that energy to entropy, and my system would slowly run down; but if I went with the flow, entered my personal chaos, let in more information and allowed it to work its magic, I would self-organize at a higher level. Somewhere in my personal chaos lay the pattern of my highest potential, a blueprint of my future self.

In the last ten years, I have discovered that menopause is a time of great transformation. It plunges our bodies, as well as our minds, into chemical chaos. As estrogen wanes, the right hemisphere of our brain becomes more active. We access more of our creativity, our aesthetic sense, our intuition. We shift from a linear mode of thought to a spatial one, in which we perceive relationships within wholeness.

While our bodies are preparing for spiritual adulthood, our psyches are challenged to grow. Change happens. Growth is what we make of it. Menopause is a time to look back upon the past, to reflect, to digest, to gather the lessons, harvest the wisdom and understand the significance of our lives. It is a time to make peace with the past and release it. Our Souls don't want us to cling to fading memories. They urge us to use the rich harvest of life experience to nourish ourselves, our loved ones, our community, our world. We are meant to realize our destiny, to become Spiritual Adults, to assume responsibility for our passion and let it guide us to our highest potential. We are meant to become the wise ones, mentors to those who follow.

At menopause, if we make the most of our change, if we face our fear and enter chaos willingly, we can use its power to discover our own pattern of unfolding beauty. We can align with the Strange Attractor of our own highest potential and be drawn forth by its power. What are the Strange Attractors in our lives? The possibilities are endless. They could be our worst fears, as of disease, dementia, loneliness, despair; or our brightest dreams and visions, our passion and creativity, our sense of meaning and the fulfillment of destiny. All this potential lies in chaos. We have the power to choose.

Menopause is an initiation, a beginning. We will spend the rest of our lives building upon this foundation. The process bestows upon us the tools and resources we need to fulfill the commitment of spiritual adulthood. Every challenge we encounter during our rite of passage rewards us with a gift, a virtue of character: courage from facing fear; strength from grief; compassion through self-knowledge and suffering; wisdom through examining our lives and harvesting the lessons;

power from integrity; freedom from responsibility; grace from the Light. As menopause molds our character, we evolve our living relationship with the Divine. We grow beyond a spirituality of childhood obedience and adolescent rebellion into the co-creation of spiritual adulthood.

When we commit to living the light of our spiritual potential, our "golden" years will glow with fulfillment. The more love we radiate into our world, the more will reflect back to us. The more gratitude we feel and share, the more we'll have to be grateful for. The more joy we express creatively, the more joyous and creative our world will become. In short, as we send our light forth into the world, the world becomes illumined.

We each have our own unique destiny. Joseph Campbell used to say, "Follow your bliss." Our bliss lies in our passion, the passion that has been smoldering in the depths of Soul waiting for us to grow up. Once discovered, passion will sweep us effortlessly into our destiny.

Destiny doesn't need to be huge. We aren't all meant to find the cure for cancer, discover the key to world peace, or save the whales. We each contribute in the way that is best suited to our individual gifts, talents, and experience. No act of Love is irrelevant. What does your Soul long for? Go after it. Let your passion inform your dream. Dream the most wonderful future for yourself and your world. Let your dream become the Strange Attractor that draws you into its fulfillment.

Paradoxically, as we each fulfill our personal destiny, we also fulfill a collective one. Our generation is the largest in history and has had a profound impact upon the world. Before we became yuppies, the bouncing babies of the '40s and '50s were the marchers and protesters of the '60s and the hippies of the '70s. We challenged consensus beliefs and behaviors on all fronts. Now we face the spectre of Age. It is our destiny to transform age as well, to restore the respect humanity once held for the wisdom and compassion of its elders.

Beyond transforming the face of age, we have the power to change the world. Herein lies a paradox. Humanity evolves through the enlightenment of its individuals. The collective transforms One by One by One. As we each discover our potential, as we develop a vision of the most positive future for ourselves and allow ourselves to be drawn into it, we transform the fabric of society.

We are the first generation with the opportunity to tap the spiritual potential of menopause. Millions of us stand upon the threshold of initiation. We are all connected in a complex, intricate web. As we meet the challenges of menopause, One by One by One we will become enlightened Spiritual Adults, paving the way for the evolution of human consciousness in the new millennium. If the flap of a butterfly wing in Brazil can create a tornado in Texas, imagine what an enlightened generation of women can do!

E L L E N   W A T E R S T O N

For the last ten years, Ellen Waterston has worked as a freelance professional writer and teacher of writing. Her articles and essays have appeared in many local and national newspapers and magazines. Ellen's poetry has appeared in Oregon East, Fishtrap Anthology #8, Clearwater Journal, Bird in Hand, West Wind Review, *and Finishing Line Press's 1999* Anthology of American Poets. *A selection of her work will appear in the upcoming anthology,* A Trek Through Eastern Oregon By Poet. *A short story was a finalist for the 1999 Heekin Foundation Tara Fellowship. An essay was one of ten selected by the Oregon Quarterly Summer 2000 competition. She was the 1998 recipient of a Fishtrap Fellowship in poetry, and in 1999 completed a three-week poetry fellowship at the Atlantic Center for the Arts in Florida. She is the author of two children's books—*Tea at Miss Jean's *and* Barney's Joy. *Ellen is currently working on a creative nonfiction project. A New Englander who moved to the ranching West, her work is rooted in both of these cultural and geographic landscapes.*

Girlfriends and Baboons

I'm a little concerned that it will turn out I know more about baboons than I think I do. That there really are parallels between how my girl-friends and I behave and how baboons behave. I like to keep a respectful distance from our hairy ancestors. I mean—we're far more sophisticated, right? We've come a long way, baby, right? It's just that when my girlfriends and I get together for our annual weekend retreat, I'm not so sure.

As I am the only one of the five who hasn't ended up living back in the Northeast, where we're all from, we generally hold our annual meeting in New England. We all went to college together. We are now all fifty-plus years old. We've been doing this, off and on, for twenty years. The hostess for the year kicks out her children and spouse, and we take over the house for the weekend.

It starts the minute we arrive. Squeals and high-pitched shrieks of recognition. Exuberant hops up and down. The specific sub of this particular species knows instantly that these are signs of welcome—

not threatening, not territorial, not dominating. "My God!" "You made it!" "Isn't this wonderful?" But then someone inevitably squeals: "Look at you!" Each of us picks up the scent immediately. I mean immediately.

The high-pitched squeals subside and a sacred silence is observed as we all peer intently at one another, standing stock-still, barely breathing. The process of inventorying absolutely every single aspect about one another's physical presence should take longer than it does—when you think of all that we observe, and in what excruciating and shameless detail. But it doesn't take more than a minute. We've had lots of practice. It is a skill characteristic of this subgroup of mid-century female humans. It is our equivalent of the baboons' social bonding activity of removing fleas and lice—checking out haircuts, wrinkles, weight gain or loss, attempts at fashion, sagging this, bulging that. We tease the notion of surgical solutions to our aging appearance, pulling the skin back from our faces with our hands and silently offering that revised edition as a solution. Facelifts, boob jobs, vein removal, permanent mascara, the scorched skin from radiation treatment—are all dutifully noted. One gently parts the other's hair to examine the root color. Another will slowly raise her upper lip and bare her teeth, revealing a mouthful of braces.

As suddenly as the group lapsed into total silence and mutual scrutiny, we now, as if on cue, sprawl indecorously across the furniture and, with abandon, greedily devour carrot sticks, cheese, and wine. The noisy banter resumes. The grooming and physical assessment phase is over. All have verified that we are still physically familiar to one another by displaying the identifying physical attributes that secure our places in the tribe.

The next phase of the welcoming process is tribal orientation—the discussion of family members and dynamics. How goes the hunting and gathering? What social order do we subscribe to? At first, "OK." or "Fine." are all that are offered. As we delve beyond the superficial, the exchange becomes inevitably more guarded. Each one of us requires general validation and confirmation of our place in the band before too much high-risk divulging takes place. For some, that takes a while. Others exhibit stress. One might suddenly up and run in a tight circle around the whole group, engaged in a tense internal struggle about whether it is even possible to leave, despite the dictates of her bladder. The information is coming so fast, and she knows instinctively that absence at this stage of the greeting process can produce trailing raised eyebrows, a flick of the hand followed by a slow shake of the head in sympathy for her choice of a third husband, her son's drug problems. She musters up the courage and leaves to use the bathroom, but also to glance in the mirror, to make sure she looks as good as she hopes. To encourage flush back into the cheek, with a deft pinch. To give the temporary illusion of casual, windblown hair that turning the head abruptly upside-down will produce—that is, until the thinning strands settle back into uninspired flatness against the skull as she re-enters the room.

Eventually, one of the members ventures something very honest, heartfelt. That person immediately assumes the alpha role during this phase of the reacquaintance, for personal honesty and bravery, in combination, are a highly valued quality among this breed. Soon the alpha's courage is mimicked by the other women, and all begin to divulge more and more, louder and louder—their words greased by each sip of wine and by the boldness of whoever spoke just before. Soon all is known and acknowledged about husbands, personal victories, affairs, professional accomplishments, hormone replacement, children, addictions, athletic undertakings, and travels.

We eat out together at least one night, the conversations about absolutely anything flowing out onto the street, on into the taxi or subway, all over the walls and floors of the restaurant. Our talk propels us, encapsulates us. We move like a soap bubble through the air, oblivious to all except one another, our selves as reflected and confirmed by our friends. "Can I take your order?" the waiter repeats, for the fifth time.

And finally, on the last day, as we confront separation, we move to a deeper level. And here I bid the baboons farewell. We left them behind in the picked-over piles of discarded societal, professional, and personal demands on our lives. What's left are our core selves. "I long to get back to my painting." "I have taken up the piano." "I am writing every day again, now that the children are gone." "I have started training for a marathon—it's just something I've always wanted to do." "I'm going back to school."

It's not about knowing the ending. It's not about ourselves as measured by social, personal, or professional accomplishments. Do we envy the younger women we know who have put themselves relentlessly first from the outset? Our lives and personas can claim a different patina, rendered in the kiln of sacrifices we have made to children, husbands, jobs—in most instances, postponing our personal, creative expression. Those detours will make our creative expression all the more vivid, rich. That is, if we haven't altogether forgotten how to speak up—which is truly epidemic among women our age. Now, we all acknowledge, is the time. We have been pioneers in so many ways, we mid-century women—our unique profile etched by the Pill, women's liberation, Vietnam, communes, legal abortion, drugs, technology, and a powerful, male-dominated subtext that fought to keep us in a traditional mold. Let's talk, paint, sing, sculpt, and run about it.

Before saying goodbye, we stand, as we always do, in a circle, our arms draped over each other's shoulders like rugby players in a scrum, contemplating the next play. We rock back and forth as we encourage each other to reclaim what was always there, to own our ability to create whatever we desire, and to reassure one another we have all the time we need. Finally, we break up the chain of woven hearts, and amidst the exchange of shiny objects, bits of paper, hastily scrawled e-mail addresses, and other talismans such as baboons also favor, we lope off into the wilds, our arms dangling at our sides. But our knuckles don't touch the ground. Neither do our feet, for we have reminded one another that we can fly.

KIT WILSON

Kit Wilson is committed to the Grandmother archetype, the elder woman as wisdom keeper and healer, and to her role within that tradition, teaching Circle. She is a passionate student of Christina Baldwin and Ann Linnea's PeerSpirit teachings, which complement her Zen practices. A psychotherapist by training, Kit continues to work in private practice and volunteers at a hospice.
She is the editor of the Circle of Grandmothers *newsletter, and last year was a writer-in-residence at the women writers' retreat, Hedgebrook, on Whidbey Island in Washington's Puget Sound. For information regarding the annual gathering of the Council of Grandmothers, contact Judy O'Leary at gmcouncil@aol.com.*
To subscribe to Circle of Grandmothers *newsletter, contact Kit Wilson at 3907 E. Campbell, Phoenix, AZ 85018. Her e-mail address is kitw@home.com.*

Council of Grandmothers

In my mid-sixties I knew that my needs were shifting. I was moving more deeply into the process of becoming an old woman, and was looking for a different way to "do aging." I wanted to be of service. Certainly I did not want to be put on a shelf and ignored or condescended to, like my mother and her generation. But the newer version of retirement, with the housing developments walled off from the world, and the intense focus on trying to stay young, didn't suit me either. I knew I was searching, and I hungered for emotional and spiritual support. It was a "felt" need, not fully recognized or understood until I found myself involved with a group of elder women who call themselves, quite simply, *The Grandmothers*.

SNAPSHOT: *A meeting of an ongoing Grandmothers' spiritual support circle.*

It is dark-of-the-moon in Dragoon, Arizona. In the desert some distance from the village, the white domes of Shirley's

sandbag homestead reflect our candlelight, then fade into the
night as we move out onto the land. Silently we form a line,
aging hand reaching to steady aging hand. Slowly and carefully we make our way through the high desert grassland. Ten
old women. The narrow band of light from our tall candles
eerily turns the dry grass to a luminous ivory. Joey the
Samoyed appears, a pale ghost. He joins the procession and
quickly vanishes again into the darkness. Someone softly
punctuates our footsteps with a drum.

The South Rocks loom up, at first a presence more felt
than seen. Our candles begin to pick up the shapes, the
rough surfaces, the sparkling mica walls. For our ritual
tonight we have chosen a raised stone slab, a natural formation consecrated in long-ago times by Apache women. Their
grinding holes, the evidence of women's patience and
endurance, connect us—we are here to listen for their wisdom and the wisdom of this sacred land. One by one, we
place our candles in the center of the rock and quietly form a
circle around the fire. Allegra, tonight's ceremonialist, lights
copal in a conch shell, and offers the purifying smoke to each
of us, to Joey, to the stars.

Now we all begin to drum. The rhythm comes together
slowly at first, then gradually builds to a unified crescendo—
then four sharp deliberate beats—and silence. On this moon-
less night, the stars wrap us in a blanket of wonder. No one
speaks into the center. That will come later. The grass
responds to the caress of the wind with a soft murmur. Joey

rustles dry bushes as he passes. A coyote calls, far off to the east, and receives an answer. The sounds of silence.

I breathe in sharply, a shudder of excitement passing through me. Deep inside there is a knowing—I understand that for this brief moment in time, our circle is the connection, the conduit, between the mystery of the universe and the molten core of our Mother, the earth—between yesterday, today, and tomorrow.

SNAPSHOT: *Monthly meeting of the Phoenix Council of Grandmothers.*

In a house in the heart of metropolitan Phoenix, another circle is about to start. Jo and I are re-creating the space. We place eight backrests on the floor, one for each woman who will attend, and one for Glorianne, who will be missing tonight. Lovingly removing the objects from the storage box, we carefully arrange them in the center. A now-familiar blue batik scarf serves as altar cloth. Then come four candles— one for each direction. Each woman has contributed an object that has meaning for her. And over the years our centerpiece has acquired other things that are now part of our collective story. We unpack these, and when the box is empty Jo adds the fresh flowers she brought from her garden. Finally, we place the talking piece—a root from an old tree, battered by floods, dried by desert drought, but still clinging to life by a slim thread when I claimed it—respectfully, as a symbol of our circle.

After our hugs of greeting, we smudge each other with the purifying smoke of California sage, and take our seats. A moment of silence, the sound of a bell, a few simple words, and our circle is closed. Barbara takes the talking stick. Her mother has developed Alzheimer's disease. Barbara and her sister recently made the painful decision to move their mom to a place equipped to deal with her intensifying symptoms. This week they have been cleaning out her house—sorting through a lifetime of memories, trying to decide what, if anything, to save. Barbara says, "When I move, I'm going to get rid of everything. I don't want my children to have to go through this. I'm not keeping any junk." She sounds angry. She talks about how painful it is to sort through drawers of clean plastic grocery bags, each carefully rolled and fastened by a rubber band; to find the yellowed scraps of paper with recipes from her childhood, the quantities reflecting the large farm family, grown now and scattered, but no recipes for one woman living in an empty house alone. "She kept every report card we ever brought home. She even kept her old false teeth," Barbara says, tears coming now.

We listen silently, honoring her pain, identifying. Someone says, "I'm thinking about all the stuff I have in my house—what I wouldn't want my kids to find." We are quiet again. "Well," I say, "I'm pretty sure I don't want them to find the vibrator in my nightstand drawer." Everyone laughs. Someone asks, "So what if they do? Maybe they'll love it!"

As the talking stick moves from hand to hand, our reflections turn to recent violent news that has been flooding the media—the U.S. choice to use bombs to stop a war in a far-away country, the stories of children killing children here at home. We express our grief and our despair and, finally, the possibility of hope. We are not women who think we know the answers. But we each, in our own way and despite our age, try in our daily lives to make some contribution to our communities and our families. We come together in this circle each month to witness and support one another as we try to find new ways to use our years of experience.

The Grandmothers originated in the head and heart of Mary Diamond, a seventy-five-year-old woman of vision and an exceptional networker. Mary loved the Native American saying, "When the grandmothers speak, the world will heal." Thinking it would be a wonderful motto for elders seeking a new model for aging, she decided to explore this idea.

Mary called the first Council of Grandmothers in October 1994, in the week of the full moon. I was one of sixteen elder women invited to attend. We lived in community for a week at Mary's small retreat center in Southern Arizona. As we sat in council in the grandmothers' yurt and slept together in one house, most of us in the same room, we discovered that despite our differences we shared similar values and world views. We felt deeply about the earth; we were concerned for the viability and sustainability of all living things; we embraced diversity, encouraged tolerance, and welcomed the wisdom of indigenous teachers. We were open to the idea of conscious aging and the notion of preparing for death. We believed that the sacred is a part of everyday life.

Mary's intention, and our task in that first council, was to reflect on the words, "When the grandmothers speak, the world will heal." To ask ourselves: What does that mean for me, in my life? How do I prepare to be an elder? How do I bring my wisdom forward into the world? What can we do collectively? What must we do alone? How can we support each other?

There was no real road map for our council, although our use of ritual and a talking stick had a flavor of earth-based spirituality. We told our stories and sang our songs, wrote poetry, drummed and danced, meditated, and tried to figure out how best to use the energy we were creating. We wrote a letter to President Clinton asking that he pay attention when a grandmother speaks.

We were all a little surprised at how close we felt after one short week. We hadn't known how badly we needed one another. It was magical—the silence, the ceremony, the connecting of head and heart. We left believing that our closing circle was a beginning, not an end.

Mary Diamond's idea was that the Council of Grandmothers would continue to convene in the week of the full moon in October for at least five years. She believed that more and more women would come each year, and that from the large gatherings small circles of women would form, bringing grandmother wisdom forward into the world.

Many of Mary's hopes have been realized. Following that first gathering, ten of us formed a spiritual support circle that continues to meet for two days every other month. For the first five years, this circle, which included Mary, also served as a steering and planning committee for the annual gatherings.

Since 1994, the Arizona Grandmothers has grown into a loose network of older women from almost every U.S. state, Canada, Germany, England, and Wales. The annual council in October draws between fifty and seventy-five women, with ages ranging from forty-five to 100. The *Circle of Grandmothers*, a bimonthly newsletter, has a mailing list of over 400 names. Small circles birthed at the October gatherings are springing up across the country. We have been called a growing "movement," although "movement" seems too grand a label for something so purposely fluid and lacking in definition. You can subscribe to the newsletter, and there is, of course, a fee for the October conference. But there is no official organization, nothing to join, and there is strong interest in keeping it that way.

Our Arizona-based core group consists of women from diverse backgrounds and traditions. Cora is still teaching dance at eighty-two and is an activist for nonviolence, willing to go to jail if necessary for what she believes. Shirley and Allegra share fifteen acres in southeastern Arizona. Their tiny stuccoed homes are constructed of sandbags, an innovative alternative housing idea that draws a constant stream of visitors. Sister Virginia, a retired nun, lives near them and opens her house to anyone needing a temporary retreat. Barrie, a retired teacher, lives in an adobe house in Tucson, is a poet, and has been a hospice volunteer for more than twenty years. Ruth writes, and since her husband died she has decided to move into a co-housing project. Nancy mentors inner-city girls as they prepare for their coming-of-age rites of passage.

Being a biological grandmother isn't a requirement—many women have neither married nor had children. What draws us together is a shared energy—a mix of spiritual aliveness, similar values, and a desire to make a difference.

Who we are shows up in the newsletter. In it we tell our stories. The story of the three Grandmothers living on the Mexican border who, one stormy winter day, provided food and shelter for thirty hungry and exhausted Mexican nationals. The story of a Grandmother who used her home to operate an afternoon program for inner-city kids. The tale of the Grandmother who sits alone in a simple cabin on a mountaintop in Oregon meditating and praying for peace. One Grandmother writes about her Permaculture workshops. Another tells about the Raging Grannies, a group of Canadian women who stage a demonstration whenever they feel the environment, children, or human rights are being threatened. Recently a Grandmother wrote about her dispute with a hospital billing department. She ended up challenging the hospital administration and the Medicare bureaucracy. And she won!

The Grandmothers attend to death and the process of dying respectfully and unflinchingly. From the beginning, we have been aware that all of us have limited time. Once again, Mary Diamond led the way. Mary died of cancer in 1997. From her diagnosis in early August through her death in late September, the Grandmothers in our small circle supported her and her daughters. And Mary showed us how to say *yes*, even in the final weeks of life, even to death.

Although we invent and refine as we go, the Grandmother gatherings in October have developed a unique style. They are held in Arizona in natural settings, never in hotels. There is always a full-moon ceremony and other rituals that honor the earth. Leadership and workshop offerings come from the network. We do not pay presenters.

Each year we emphasize the use of the circle as a form that is congruent with our vision of "the grandmothers speaking so the world will heal." At each gathering, we spend time teaching the form, guided by the principles explicated in Christina Baldwin's book, *Calling the Circle*. We find that participants best bond with one another when they are grouped in small circles that meet once a day. We also believe that the deepest work we can do, be it environmental-social activism or spiritual-emotional support, is most effective when using this ancient form of council. A part of our intention is to teach specific circle skills, so that women leaving the gathering will be prepared to start their own small circles when they return home.

The positive response to the October Council of Grandmothers and the *Circle of Grandmothers* newsletter has been an exciting and interesting phenomenon. Since the Grandmothers don't advertise, the results are almost entirely due to women's word-of-mouth networking. Younger women, baby boomers eager to find a model for their own transition into the later years, actively seek us out. Women in their forties and early fifties will often offer service simply for the chance to be in our company.

"The Grandmothers" is too "young" for any assessments about future growth or durability. Only time will tell. Perhaps these circles of older women, coming together, supporting each other, and speaking their truth into their communities, will, in fact, facilitate positive changes. What we do know is that we have learned that we need one another and that there is power and comfort in the work we do together. We know that coming together in a sacred way to honor the earth, celebrate our years, and grieve the wounds of our culture has provided us with inspiration and a feeling that we are not alone. My late sixties were the best years of my life, and despite an increase in aches and pains, I am looking forward to my seventies being just as good. I attribute much of this to the Grandmothers. If we have not yet managed to heal the world, we are certainly working hard at healing ourselves.

Other Books from Beyond Words Publishing, Inc.

Adult

THE SECOND WIVES CLUB
Secrets for Becoming Lovers for Life
Authors: Lenore Fogelson Millian, Ph.D., and
Stephen Jerry Millian, Ph.D.
$14.95, softcover

Are you or someone you know a second wife? Are you tired of arguing about your husband's first marriage? *The Second Wives Club* is the book you've been waiting for. Join the Club and learn the six secrets of successful second marriages. Learn how you can have wedded bliss while avoiding the pitfalls that second marriages bring. Don't be put off by his ex-wife. Help him get rid of his old "baggage" and make space in your relationship to be lovers for life. Includes chapters on how to deal with the first wife, the children, the grandchildren, the mother-in-law, the friends, and the memories.

THE WOMAN'S BOOK OF DREAMS
Dreaming as a Spiritual Practice
Author: Connie Cockrell Kaplan; Foreword: Jamie Sams
$14.95, softcover

Dreams are the windows to your future and the catalysts to bringing the new and creative into your life. Everyone dreams. Understanding the power of dreaming helps you achieve your greatest potential with ease. *The Woman's Book of Dreams* emphasizes the uniqueness of women's dreaming and shows the reader how to dream with intention, clarity, and focus. In addition, this book will teach you how to recognize the thirteen types of dreams, how your monthly cycles affect your dreaming, how the moon's position in the sky and its relationship to your astrological chart determine your dreaming, and how to track your dreams and create a personal map of your dreaming patterns. Connie Kaplan guides you through an ancient woman's group form called dream circle—a sacred space in which to share dreams with others on a regular basis. Dream circle allows you to experience life's mystery by connecting with other dreamers. It shows you that through dreaming together with your circle, you create the reality in which you live. It is time for you to recognize the power of dreams and to put yours into action. This book will inspire you to do all that—and more.

THE INTUITIVE WAY

A Guide to Living from Inner Wisdom
Author: Penney Peirce; Foreword: Carol Adrienne
$16.95, softcover

When intuition is in full bloom, life takes on a magical, effortless quality; your world is suddenly full of synchronicities, creative insights, and abundant knowledge just for the asking. *The Intuitive Way* shows you how to enter that state of perceptual aliveness and integrate it into daily life to achieve greater natural flow through an easy-to-understand, ten-step course. Author Penney Peirce synthesizes teachings from psychology, East-West philosophy, religion, metaphysics, and business. In simple and direct language, Peirce describes the intuitive process as a new way of life and demonstrates many practical applications from speeding decision-making to expanding personal growth. Whether you're just beginning to search for a richer, fuller life experience or are looking for more subtle, sophisticated insights about your spiritual path, *The Intuitive Way* will be your companion as you progress through the stages of intuition development.

PRIDE AND JOY

The Lives and Passions of Women Without Children
Author: Terri Casey
$14.95, softcover

Pride and Joy is an enlightening collection of first-person interviews with twenty-five women who have decided not to have children. This book shatters the stereotypes that surround voluntarily childless women—that they are self-centered, immature, workaholic, unfeminine, materialistic, child-hating, cold, or neurotic. Diversity is a strong suit of this book. The narrators range in age from twenty-six-year-old Sarah Klein, who teaches second grade in an inner-city public school, to eighty-two-year-old Ruby Burton, a retired court reporter who grew up in a mining camp. The women talk about their family histories, intimate relationships, self-images, creative outlets, fears, ambitions, dreams, and connections to the next generation. Even though these women are not mothers, many voluntarily childless women help to raise and sometimes rescue the next generation while retaining the personal freedom they find so integral to their identities.

TEACH ONLY LOVE

The Twelve Principles of Attitudinal Healing

Author: Gerald G. Jampolsky, M.D.

$12.95, softcover

From best-selling author Dr. Gerald Jampolsky comes a revised and expanded version of one of his classic works, based on *A Course in Miracles*. In 1975, Dr. Jampolsky founded the Center for Attitudinal Healing, a place where children and adults with life-threatening illnesses could practice peace of mind as an instrument of spiritual transformation and inner healing—practices that soon evolved into an approach to life with profound benefits for everyone. This book explains the twelve principles developed at the Center, all of which are based on the healing power of love, forgiveness, and oneness. They provide a powerful guide that allows all of us to heal our relationships and bring peace and harmony to every aspect of our lives.

FORGIVENESS

The Greatest Healer of All

Author: Gerald G. Jampolsky, M.D.; Foreword: Neale Donald Walsch

$12.95, softcover

Forgiveness: The Greatest Healer of All is written in simple, down-to-earth language. It explains why so many of us find it difficult to forgive and why holding on to grievances is really a decision to suffer. The book describes what causes us to be unforgiving and how our minds work to justify this. It goes on to point out the toxic side effects of being unforgiving and the havoc it can play on our bodies and on our lives. But above all, it leads us to the vast benefits of forgiving.

The author shares powerful stories that open our hearts to the miracles which can take place when we truly believe that no one needs to be excluded from our love. Sprinkled throughout the book are Forgiveness Reminders that may be used as daily affirmations supporting a new life free of past grievances.

Children's

GIRLS KNOW BEST
Advice for Girls from Girls on Just About Everything
Editor: Michelle Roehm
$8.95, softcover

Girls Know Best contains the writings of thirty-eight different girls from across the United States. The book is divided into chapters focusing on specific issues and giving advice from the girl writers to the girl readers. The topics include living with siblings, school/homework, parents, divorce, and dealing with stepfamilies, boys, friends, losses when your best friend moves away or you do, depression, dealing with differences (race and religion), drugs, our bodies and looks, and overcoming life's biggest obstacles. Each writing includes a photo of the girl author and a brief background about her and her dreams. Breaking up these chapters are fun activities that girls can do together or by themselves, including best-friend crafts, ways kids can save the environment, ideas for volunteering, natural beauty fun, and even how to pass notes in class without getting caught. The book is a vehicle for encouraging girls to use their creativity and to believe in themselves and their infinite potential. By showing that any girl can do it, our girl authors will be models and inspirations for all girls.

GIRLS WHO ROCKED THE WORLD

Heroines from Sacagawea to Sheryl Swoopes

Author: Amelie Welden

$8.95, softcover

Girls Who Rocked the World, a companion book to the *Girls Know Best* series, encourages girls to believe in themselves and go for their dreams. It tells the stories of thirty-five real girls, past and present, from all around the world, who achieved amazing feats and changed history *before reaching their twenties.* Included are well-known girls like Helen Keller and Sacagawea as well as many often-overlooked heroines such as Joan of Arc, Phillis Wheatley, and Wang Yani. Interspersed along with the stories of heroines are photos and writings of real girls from all over America answering the question, "How do I plan to rock the world?" By highlighting the goals and dreams of these girls, the book links these historical heroines to girls today who will be the next ones to rock the world!

To order or to request a catalog, contact

Beyond Words Publishing, Inc.

20827 N.W. Cornell Road, Suite 500

Hillsboro, OR 97124-9808

503-531-8700 or 1-800-284-9673

You can also visit our Web site at *www.beyondword.com* or e-mail us at *info@beyondword.com.*

It's Your Turn Next Time Contest

Wanted: The Wisdom and Experience of Women over Fifty!
Beyond Words Publishing, Inc., invites you to participate in the next book of permission and promise for women over fifty. Whatever freedom you seek to celebrate, whatever story you wish to speak honestly about—your voice could join the voices of other (extra)ordinary women who are redefining aging and claiming a new vitality for the years past fifty.

What to Send Us
Please send your complete essay (five to seven pages long and double spaced), your biography (no longer than one page), and a self-addressed stamped envelope. Only hard copy (paper) submissions will be accepted.

Deadline for Entries: October 1, 2000
Writers will be notified of acceptance by January 15, 2001.

Send Submissions to
It's Your Turn Next Time Contest
Beyond Words Publishing, Inc.
20827 N.W. Cornell Road, Suite 500
Hillsboro, OR 97124-9808
503-531-8700

For more information, contact Adult Acquisitions
adultacquisitions@beyondword.com

Beyond Words Publishing, Inc.

OUR CORPORATE MISSION:

Inspire to Integrity

OUR DECLARED VALUES:

We give to all of life as life has given us.

We honor all relationships.

Trust and stewardship are integral to fulfilling dreams.

Collaboration is essential to create miracles.

Creativity and aesthetics nourish the soul.

Unlimited thinking is fundamental.

Living your passion is vital.

Joy and humor open our hearts to growth.

It is important to remind ourselves of love.

Our Turn, Our Time